IMO OLYMPIAD WORKBOOK 2

SOF INTERNATIONAL MATHEMATICS OLYMPIAD 2023-24

SANAGE EDITORIAL BOARD

SANAGE
PUBLISHING HOUSE

Contents

CHAPTER 1

NUMBER SENSE

TOPICS COVERED:

* Numerals and Number Names (3 digit)
* Arranging numbers in ascending and descending order
* Expanded form
* Formation of numbers (with/without repetition)from given digits information
* Comparing Numbers
* Sheet and place value
* Even and odd numbers

MATHEMATICAL REASONING

1. **The place value of digit 5 in 577 is ___**

   A) 50   B) 500   C) 5   D) 55

2. **Which of the following number names are not shown on the monitor?**

   A) Nine hundred seven

   B) Seven hundred twelve

   C) Four hundred seventy one

   D) Three hundred forty four

3. **Which number is more than 200 but less than 400 present on the box?**

   A) 100   B) 390

   C) 450   D) 500

4. **Which sheet shows 347?**

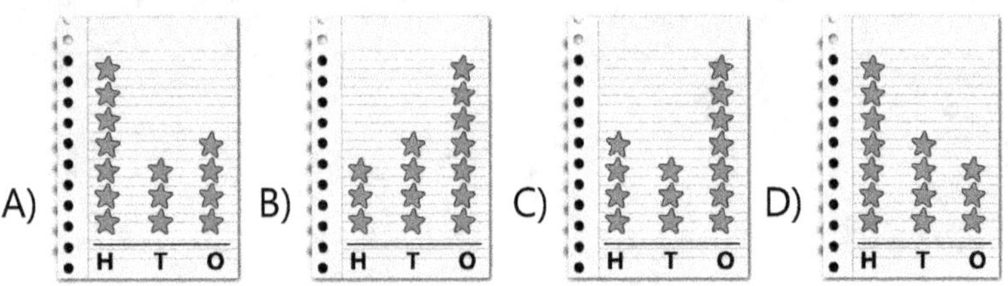

A)   B)   C)   D)

5. **Which of the following is largest 3-digit odd number ?**

    A) 086   B) 259   C) 153   D) 023

6. **Which of the following numbers is the second smallest in the group?**

    114, 255, 198, 314, 422

    A) 314   B) 114   C) 198   D) 255

7. **Which of the following number belong to the given collection of numbers?**

    A) Three hundred forty one

    B) Two hundred seventy one

    C) Four hundred twelve

    D) one hundred eighty

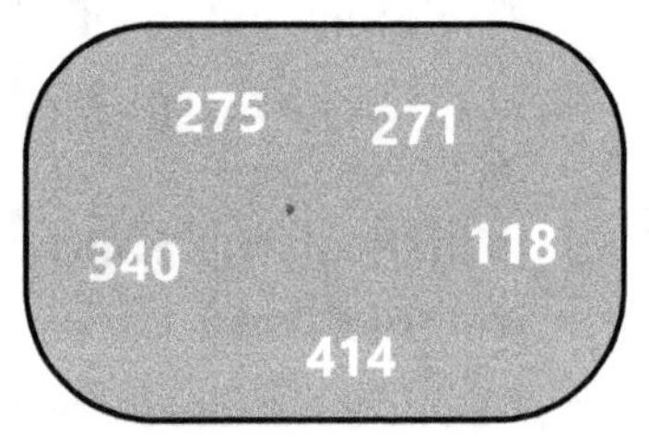

8. **80 tens is _____ 9 hundreds.**

    A) Greater than   B) Equal to   C) Less than   D) Can't say

9. **When written in number, five hundred and seven is same as _____.**

    A) 578   B) 507   C) 570   D) 577

10. **Which number is largest three digit number?**

    A) 999   B) 1000   C) 919   D) 900

11. **Which cloud has the smallest number?**

12. Which of the following number is more than 40 tens?

A) 400   B) 550   C) 325   D) 350

13. Which bowl shows the number name given below?

Five hundred fifty five

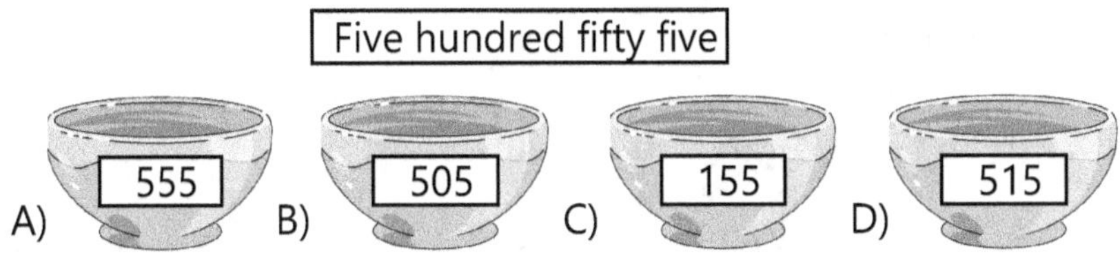

14. Smallest three digit number is ____.

A) 100   B) 01   C) 101   D) 99

15. Nine hundreds and nine in numbers is____.

A) 999   B) 990   C) 909   D) 919

16. Select the CORRECT match.

A) One hundred fifty one - 150

B) Three hundred and thirty two - 313

C) Five hundred and six - 566

D) Two hundred and twelve - 212

17. Which kite shows the smallest value?

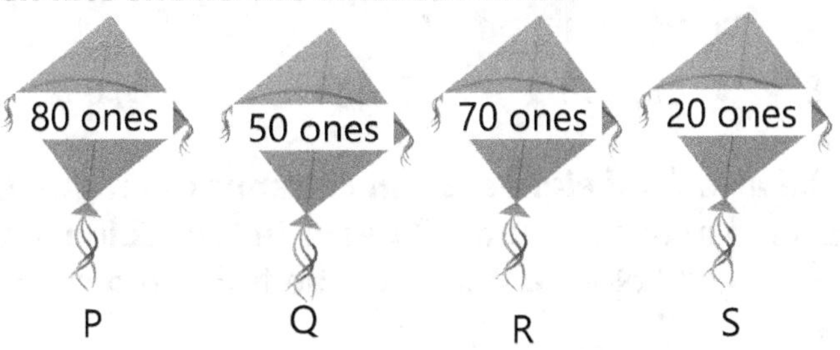

A) P   B) Q   C) S   D) R

18. **Which of the following correctly shows decreasing order of the following set of numbers?**

    A) 590, 579, 552, 535

    B) 590, 579, 535, 552

    C) 552, 535, 590, 579

    D) 590, 552, 579, 535

19. **In 561, the digit ___ is at tens place.**

    A) 6   B) 5   C) 1   D) None of these

20. **Which of the following set of numbers are arranged in decreasing order.**

    A) 818, 835, 875, 855   B) 818, 835, 855, 875

    C) 818, 855, 835, 875   D) 875, 835, 818, 855

EVERYDAY MATHEMATICS

21. **Simran has baked some muffins. The number of muffins baked by her are less than 250. Which of the following cannot be the number of muffins baked by her?**

    A) 200   B) 220   C) 160   D) 255

22. **Sujata has the set of number cards 5 8 2 Which is the smallest possible 3-digit number that can be formed by using each box only once?**

    A) 582   B) 258   C) 528   D) 852

23. **Radha arranged eight stars in columns of an sheet. She puts one bead in ones column, 3 beads in tens colum and 4 beads in hundresd column. Which of the following can be Radha's sheet?**

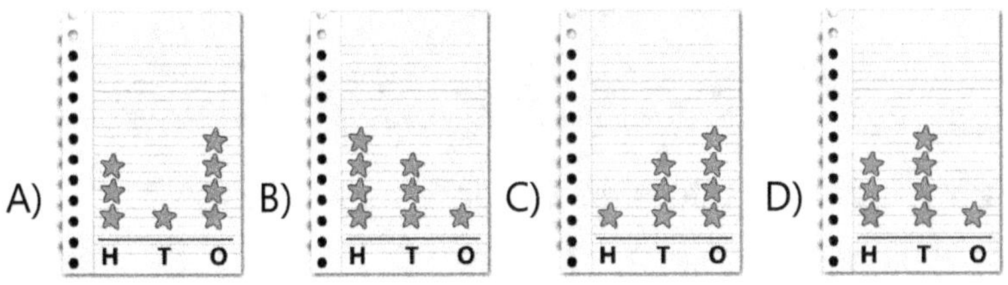

24. **The following table shows the number of toys each child have.**

Children	Number of toys
Sayali	52 ones
Poonam	3 tens 8 ones
Anil	25 tens
Shiv	8 tens 3 ones

Which of the following statement is INCORRECT?

A) Poonam has least numbers of toys.

B) Anil has maximum number of toys.

C) Shiv has 83 toys.

D) Sayali has maximum numbers of toys.

25. **The below diagram shows the number of banana's eaten by each monkey in a month.**

Which monkey ate three hundred twenty two banana's.

A) Monty

B) Gullu

C) Jacky

D) Bunny

26. Which of the following statements is CORRECT?

A) 60 ones is same as 600.

B) There are 2 ones 325.

C) The place value of 9 is 975 in 900.

D) The smallest three digit number formed by using the digits 3, 4, 2 each only ones 243.

27. Fill in the blanks.

1. Two less than the largest 3-digit numbers is __P__.

2. 50 ones = __Q__.

3. Six hundred and twenty two is same as __R__.

	P	Q	R
A)	100	550	612
B)	909	525	612
C)	999	500	620
D)	997	50	622

28. Arrange the given numbers in decreasing order.

P: 5 hundred + 2 ones

Q: 2 hundred + 3 tens + 4 ones

R: 9 hundred + 3 ones

S: 1 hundred + 5 tens + 3 ones

A) S, Q ,R, P   B) R, P, Q, S   C) R, P, S, Q   D) S, Q, P, R

29. Meera lost her purse. Use the given clues to find Meera's purse.

Clue 1: The place value of 5 in the number is 50.

Clue 2: The place value of 7 in the number is 700.

Clue 3: The digit at ones place is smallest one digit number.

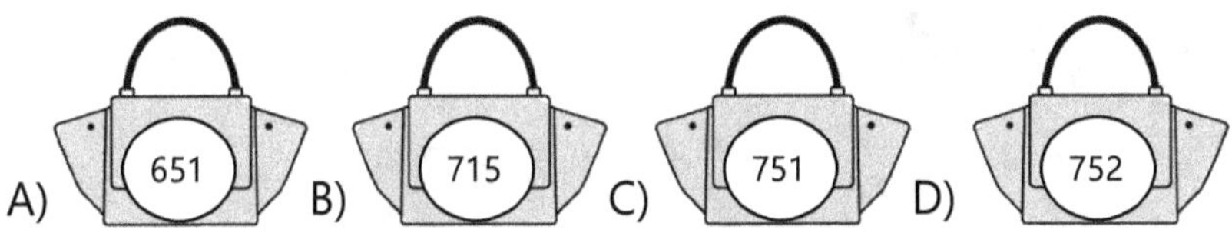

A)   B)   C)   D)

30. Which of the following balance is INCORRECT?

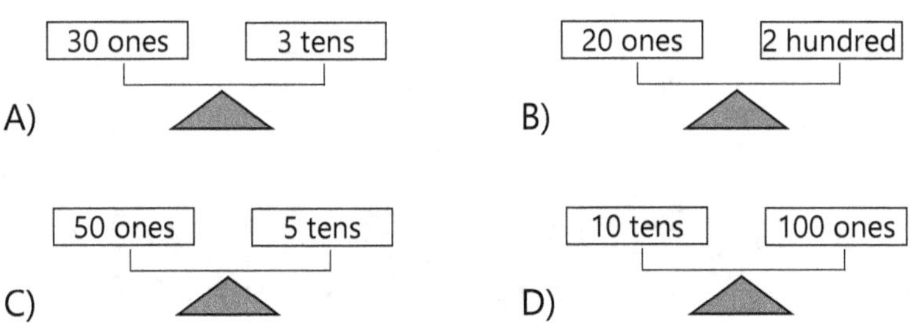

A)   B)

C)   D)

Colour your choice with color pencil				
1	**2**	**3**	**4**	**5**
A B C D	A B C D	A B C D	A B C D	A B C D
6	**7**	**8**	**9**	**10**
A B C D	A B C D	A B C D	A B C D	A B C D
11	**12**	**13**	**14**	**15**
A B C D	A B C D	A B C D	A B C D	A B C D
16	**17**	**18**	**19**	**20**
A B C D	A B C D	A B C D	A B C D	A B C D
21	**22**	**23**	**24**	**25**
A B C D	A B C D	A B C D	A B C D	A B C D

COMPUTATION OPERATION

TOPICS COVERED:

* Addition/Subtraction of 2 and 3 digit numbers with/without regrouping (carry)
* Identification of correct addition and subtraction sentences based on given pictures
* Calculate the total number of objects or add a large quantity with same number using multiplication as repeated addition
* Identification of missing number in number band using addition/subtraction
* Finding the value of missing figure or symbol in figure sentence
* Word problems on addition/subtraction

MATHEMATICAL REASONING

1. **The sum of the greatest and the smallest numbers in the given glass jar is ____.**

   A) 560   B) 732

   C) 394   D) 585

2. **Which is the most suitable addition statement for the following picture ?**

   $$3+3+3+3+3$$

   A) ★★★ + ★★★ + ★★★ + ★★★ + ★★★ + ★★★

   B) ★★★ + ★★★ + ★★★

   C) ★★★ + ★★★ + ★★★ + ★★★ + ★★★

   D) ★ + ★ + ★ + ★ + ★

3. **The difference between greatest three digit number and smallest three digit number is ____.**

A) 99   B) 990   C) 100   D) 899

4.   **Select the INCORRECT option.**

A) 3 + 4 = 5 + 2   B) 20 - 7 = 5 + 5 + 3

C) 2 + 2 + 2 + 2 = 20 - 12   D) 50 - 7 = 20 + 20 + 5

5.   _______ **groups of 3 is same as 21.**

A) 7   B) 15   C) 24   D) 6

6.   **Nandita wants to choose a note whose sum is smaller than 100. Which note will she choose?**

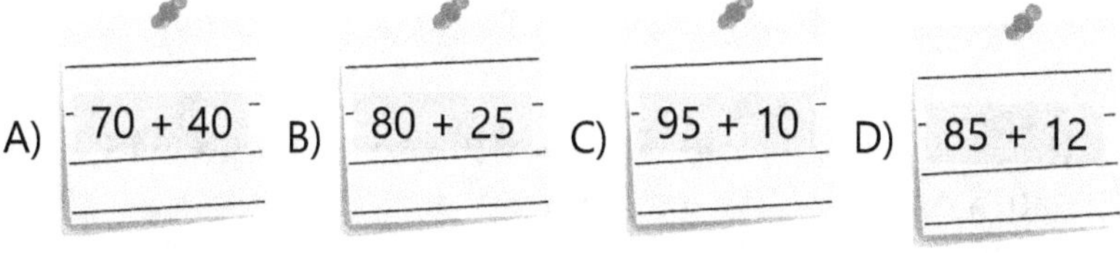

A)   B)   C)   D)

7.   **Rohan saw 4 lady bugs in a garden. How many lady bugs dots did he see in the garden?**

A) 35   B) 30

C) 32   D) 37

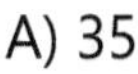

8.   **Arrange the following values from the largest to the smallest.**

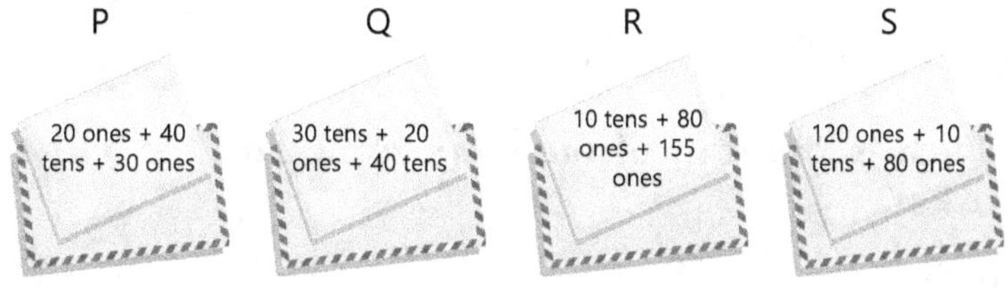

A) R, P, Q, S   B) Q, P, R, S   C) P, R, S, Q   D) S, R, P, Q

9.   **The difference between the numbers shown by two sheet ____.**

A) 80

B) 82

C) 95

D) 85

10. **Neha and her three friends shared following clips equally among themselves. How many clips did each one get?**

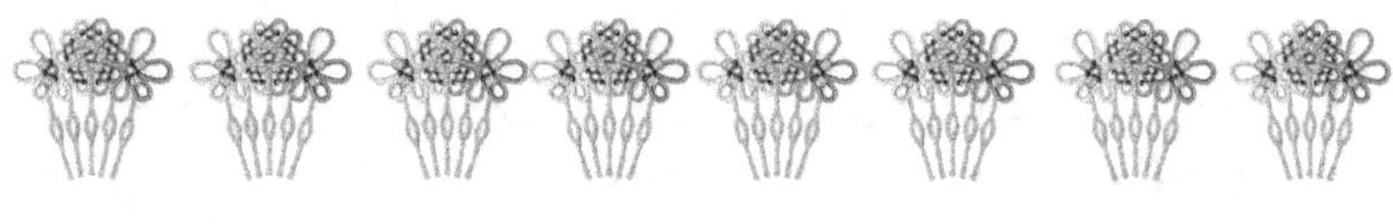

A) 8   B) 2   C) 4   D) 3

11. **If ▭ + △ + △ = 60 and triangle = 15, then the value of ▭ is _____.**

A) 20   B) 30   C) 15   D) 10

12. **Subtract a number from 100 and the result is 75. The number is ___**

A) 35   B) 25   C) 75   D) 70

13. **Which of the following subtraction sentence is based on the given picture ?**

A) 15 - 3 = 12   B) 15 - 12 = 3

C) 12 - 3 = 9   D) 12 - 9 = 3

14. **Which is the sum of numbers shown on the basket?**

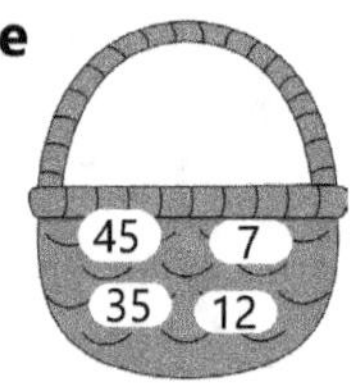

A) 95   B) 99

C) 100   D) 98

15. **I am less than 24+3 but more than 18+3. Who am I ?**

A) 16   B) 12   C) 22   D) 25

16. **In a class of 50 childrens. Each child brings 6 books and 3 pencils. How many more books are there than pencils in all?**

    A) 200   B) 150   C) 300   D) 180

17. **Sheela wants to arrange 48 cakes equally on 4 tables. Each table will have_____ cakes.**

    A) 12   B) 8

    C) 10   D) 5

18. **Riya did this subtraction problem. Which additon problem shows that she got the right answer?**

7	5
-5	3
2	2

    A) 22   B) 53   C) 53   D) 22
       +75   +75   +22   +22
       ————   ————   ————   ————

19. **Sourabh puts 8 cupcakes in each box for the sale. How many cupcakes did he use in all to put in 8 boxes?**

    A) 8   B) 65   C) 60   D) 64

20. **Sonal has 2 tins. Each tin has 6 ladoos in it. She gave 8 ladoos to her sister. How many ladoos are left with Sonal.**

    A) 8   B) 12   C) 10   D) 6

21. **Naman had 37 mangoes and Vinay had 63 mangoes. How many mangoes do they have in all?**

    A) 105   B) 100

    C) 70   D) 90

22. There were 243 childrens at the play ground. If 117 of them were girls and the rest were boys, then how many boys were there?

A) 243 - 117 B) 117+243 C) 243-217 D) 117 + 117

23. Muskan needs 378 flowers to decorate her house. She had 228 flowers in the box. How many more flowers she must buy?

A) 210 B) 100 C) 150 D) 140

24. Meena has these given cherries. If she will give two cherries to each of her five friends, then how many cherries will be left for Meena?

A) 2 B) 5

C) 4 D)6

25. There were eight ducks in the pond. How many duck legs were there in pond together ?

A) 8 B) 32

C) 12 D) 16

ACHIVERS SECTION (HOTS)

26. Find the values of R and S respectively.

A) 0, 9 B) 9, 0

C) 8, 4 D) 9, 4

```
  R   R
- S   R
-------
  R   0
```

27. Find the values of X and Y and Z respectively.

A) 25, 28, 18

B) 18, 25, 28

C) 25, 18, 28

D) 25, 15, 30

```
  X
  +
 75
  =
100
  -
 18
  =  Y  +  28  =  Z
```

28. **Identify the numer.**

A) 90   B) 82   C) 70   D) 86

29. **A shopkeeper sold twice as many cookies on Friday than on Thursday. And he sold 4 times as many cookies on Monday than on Friday. He sold 35 cookies on Thursday. How many cookies did he sell on Friday and Monday respectively?**

A) 72, 100   B) 280, 35   C) 35, 180   D) 70, 280

30. **Find the value if** ☆.

☆ + ☆ + ☆ + ☆ + ☐ + ☐ = 88   ☆ + ☆ + ☐ + ☐ = 58

A) 25   B) 15   C) 30   D) 20

Colour your choice with color pencil				
1	2	3	4	5
A B C D	A B C D	A B C D	A B C D	A B C D
6	7	8	9	10
A B C D	A B C D	A B C D	A B C D	A B C D
11	12	13	14	15
A B C D	A B C D	A B C D	A B C D	A B C D
16	17	18	19	20
A B C D	A B C D	A B C D	A B C D	A B C D
21	22	23	24	25
A B C D	A B C D	A B C D	A B C D	A B C D

LENGTH, WEIGHT, CAPACITY AND TEMPERATURE

TOPICS COVERED:

* Measuring the length using ruler
* Measuring capacity
* Measuring length, weight and capacity using their standard numbers
* Reading or measuring temperature on thermometer in C of F
* Measuring the weight using weighting scale
* Compare the lengths and weights
* Word problems

MATHEMATICAL REASONING

1. **What is the length of the longest crayon?**

   A) 10 cm

   B) 6 cm

   C) 8 cm

   D) 7 cm

   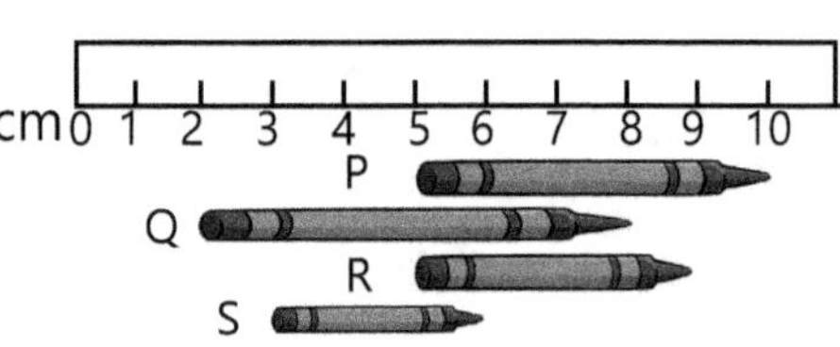

2. **Which of the following cup is the heaviest?**

   A) 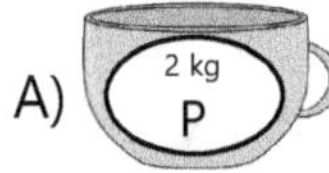

   B)

   C) 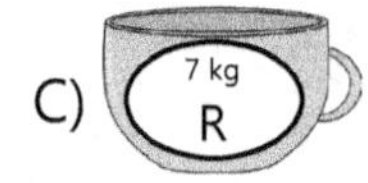

   D) 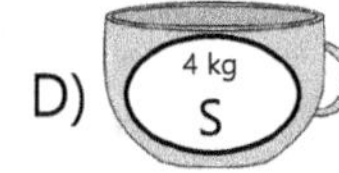

3. **If we can fill 4 glasses of milk from 1 litre milk, then we can fill 16 glasses of milk from____.**

   A) 4 litres   B) 6 litres   C) 3 litres   D) 5 litres

4. **Fridge temperature is 15°C less than the temperature shown on the given thermometer. The fridge temperarure is____**

A) 65°C

B) 45°C

C) 35°C

D) 55°C

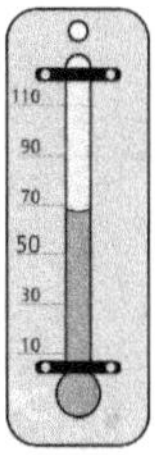

5. **The total weight of mangoes is ______ kg and melons is ____ kg.**

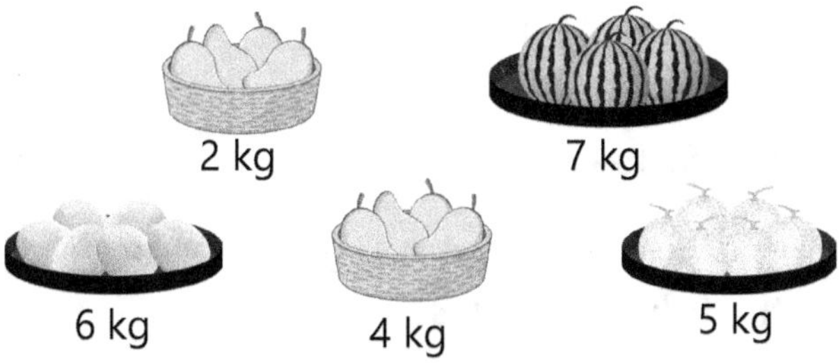

2 kg

7 kg

6 kg

4 kg

5 kg

A) 18, 6   B) 14, 5   C) 6, 18   D) 9, 15

6. **Which utensils can hold less capacity of juice?**

A) Bowl

B) Glass

C) Jug

D) None of these

7. **Which is the shortest party hat?**

A) S   B) R

C) Q   D) P

8. **Weight of 1 ball is 100 g. What is the weight of 5 such balls?**

A) 500 g   B) 200 g   C) 250 g   D) 100 g

9. **Sudhir skated from his class to market and then to home. How much distance did he cover?**

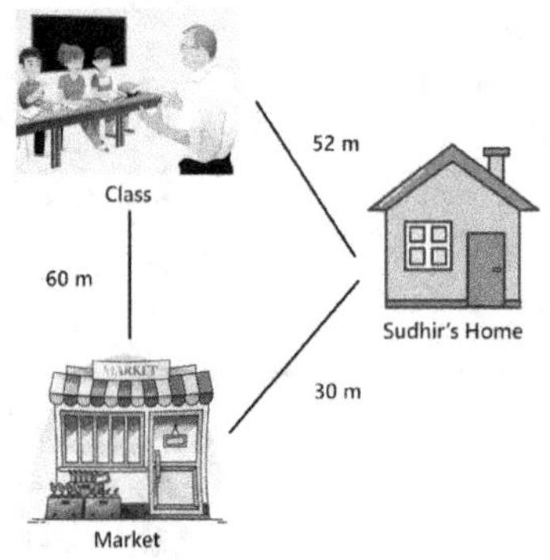

A) 110 m   B) 144 m   C) 30 m   D) 90 m

DIRECTION: (10-11): On the basis of the given figures, answer the following questions.

Rice bag   Watermelon   Books

10. **What is the total weight of watermelon and books?**

     A) 7 kg   B) 12 kg   C) 20 kg   D) 32 kg

11. **How much is rice bag heavier than books?**

     A) 4 kg   B) 2 kg   C) 5 kg   D) 3 kg

12. **How many more litres of water does the bucket can contain?**

     A) 1 litre

     B) 2 litres

     C) 5 litres

     D) 3 litres

13. **Difference between height of Giraffe and height of the Monkey is___**

A) 4 m

B) 5m

C) 8 m

D) 7 m

14. **Which bottle contains more than 300 ml of juice?**

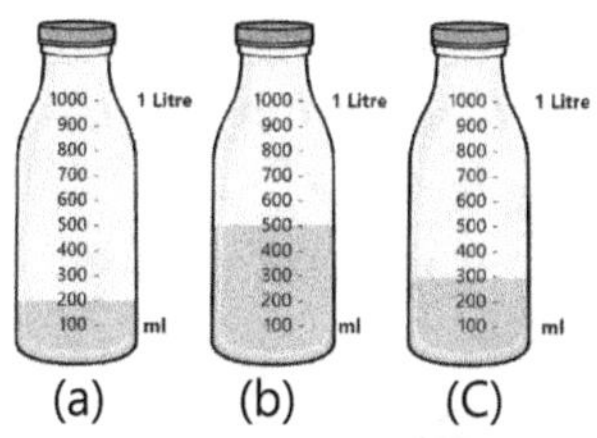

A) (a)

B) (c)

C) Both (a) and(c)

D) (b)

15. **A pot can be filled by 3 measuring jug as shown. How much water can the pot hold?**

A) 8 litres

B) 5 litres

C) 7 litres

D) 2 litres

16. **How much juice should be added to make the given quantity 10 litres?**

A) 4 litres

B) 6 litres

C) 2 litres

D) 1 litre

17. **Nitin drinks 1 litre of milk everyday. If he drinks same quantity of milk each day, how much milk does he drink in 15 days?**

A) 12 litres   B) 15 litres   C) 10 litres   D) 18 litres

18.  + + = 450 g, then 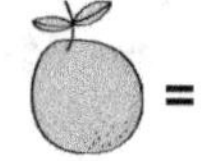 =

A) 150 g   B) 300 g   C) 100 g   D) 200 g

19. What is the height of crane (in m) shown here?

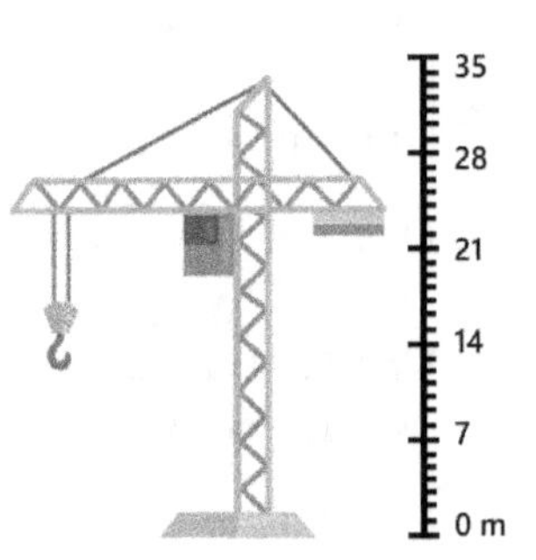

A) 105 - 63

B) 62 - 34

C) 90 - 25

D) 98 - 63

20. What is the weight of a melon?

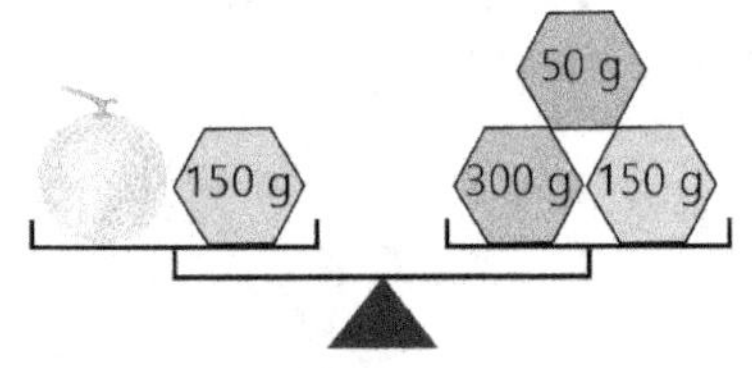

A) 250 g   B) 200 g   C) 150 g   D) 500 g

EVERYDAY MATHEMETICS

21. Rohan bought 130 litres of milk, He used 90 litres of milk for his shop. How much milk is left with him?

A) 40 litres   B) 30 litres   C) 45 litres   D) 95 litres

22. Manju baked 9 bread loafs. The weight of each bread loaf is 4 kg. What is the total weight of all the bread loafs.

A) 36 kg   B) 18 kg   C) 27 kg   D) 9 kg

23. 6 flower plants were placed at equal distance apart along one side in a ground, The distance between the first bench and the third bench is 10 m. What is the distance between the third bench and sixth bench?

A) 5 m   B) 20 m   C) 30 m   D) 15 m

24. **A tank contained 82 litres of milk. Shivani drained 35 litres of milk through a tap from from the tank. How much milk is left in the tank?**

A) 47 litres   B) 40 litres   C) 42 litres   D) 55 litres

25. **A shopkeeper has 15 bags of jowar each having weight 20 kg. What is the total weight of the jowar bags?**

A) 150 kg   B) 300 kg   C) 250 kg   D) 200 kg

ACHIVERS SECTION (HOTS)

26. **It takes 10 bowls of water to fill up the jug. It takes 2 bowls of water to fill up the tumbler. How many tumblers of water are needed to fill up the jug?**

A) 8   B) 4   C) 3   D) 7

27. **What is the weight of the pear A?**

A) 5 kg   B) 1 kg   C) 2 kg   D) 6 kg

28. **Soniya travelled from home to class. She took two routes.**

1st route: home – bookstore – class

2nd route: home – market – class

Which route was the shorter and by how much distance?

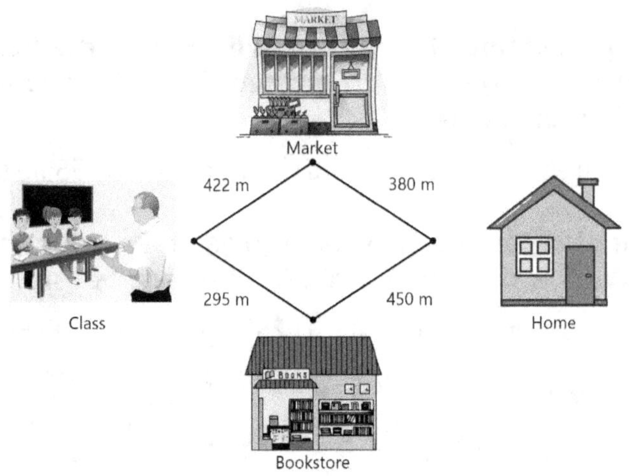

A) 2nd route, 55 mm

B) 1st route, 57 mm

C) 2nd route, 45 mm

D) 1st route, 50 mm

29. **A small milk can contains 1 litre of milk. A large milk can contains 8 litres more milk than a small milk can. Aditya bought the given milk cans. How much milk did he buy altogther?**

A) 22 litres   B) 24 litres   C) 20 litres   D) 16 litres

30. **Rice bag weight 46 kg. Jowar bag weight 10 kg less than rice bag. Wheat bag weight 5 kgs less than rice bag. Bajra bag weight 9 kg more than jowar bag. Which bag weight the most?**

A) Rice bag   B) Wheat bag   C) Jower bag   D) Bajra bag

TIME AND MONEY

MATHEMATICAL REASONING

1. Raghav starts his cricket practice from 2nd October 20XX. If he practices only on odd number of days, then how many days did he practice in October 20XX.

October 20XX						
Mon	Tue	Wed	Thu	Fri	Sat	Sun
			1	2	3	4
5	6	7	8	9	10	11
12	13	14	15	16	17	18
19	20	21	22	23	24	25
26	27	28	29	30	31	

A) 13   B) 15   C) 14   D) 16

2. Which clock shows 10 mintues past 12 : 00 p.m ?

A)    B)    C)   D) 

3. The given clock shows the time____mins after 11'o clock.

A) 10   B) 8   C) 5   D) 6

4. **The sum of five ₹ 10 notes and two ₹ 20 notes is ___.**

   A) ₹ 70   B) ₹ 90   C) ₹ 45   D) ₹ 100

5. **How many ₹ 5 coins you need to make ₹ 35?**

   A) 7   B) 5   C) 4   D) 6

6. **A clock is 10 mins fast. What is the actual time, if it is showing 8:30 p.m?**

   A) 8:20 p.m.   B) 8:10 p.m.   C) 8:40 p.m.   D) 8:25 p.m.

7. **Reena left her home in the morning at the time shown in the clock, She waited 10 mintues for the bus and reached office at 9:40 a.m. what was the duration of her journey?**

   A) 1 hour 10 minutes

   B) 1 hour

   C) 55 minutes

   D) 30 minutes

8. **Samir started walking to the class at 3:45 p.m. He reached the class at 4:05 p.m, How long did he take to walk to the class?**

   A) 15 minutes   B) 20 minutes   C) 25 minutes   D) 30 minutes

   DIRECTION (9-11): The cost of few items are given below, now answer the given question.

1 Glue bottle ₹ 10

1 Pencil box ₹ 25

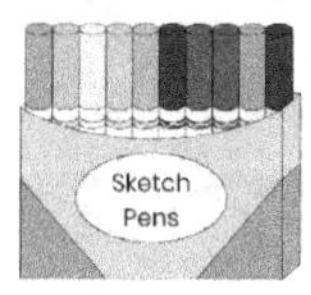

1 Sketch pen box ₹ 30

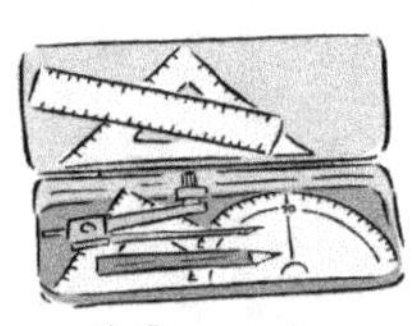

1 Geometry box ₹ 40

9. **Which is the most costliest item?**

A) 1 Pencil box   B) 1 Geometry box

C) 1 Glue bottle   D) 1 Sketch pen box

10. **If Mona has ₹ 10, then which of the following items can she buy?**

A) 1 Geometry box   B) 1 Pencil box

C) 1 Sketch pen box   D) 1 Glue bottle

11. **How much money is required to buy all the items?**

A) ₹ 110   B) ₹ 116   C) ₹ 105   D) ₹ 150

12. **Which set of money is ENOUGH to buy the given bag?**

13. **A clock is 5 mins slow. If the clock is showing 12:30 p.m. then what is the actual time?**

A) 12:40 p.m.   B) 12:35 p.m.   C) 12:25 p.m.   D)12:15 p.m.

14. **Count the number of rupees Ravi has.**

A) ₹ 105   B) ₹ 100   C) ₹ 110   D) ₹ 115

15. **What is the time if is 10 mins after 12 noon?**

   A) 12:10 p.m.   B) 11:40 a.m.   C) 12:00 p.m.   D)12:10 a.m.

16. **Varun studys in the class from 4:00 p.m to 5:30 p.m. How long did he studys?**

   A) 1 hr 35 mins   B) 2 hr 30 mins

   C) 1 hr 30 mins   D) 1 hr

DIRECTON (17-18): A pair of sandals costs ₹ 180 and a Shirt costs ₹ 150. Now, answer the folllwoing questions.

₹ 150   ₹ 180

17. **How much will 2 similar pairs of sandals cost?**

   A) ₹ 360   B) ₹ 150   C) ₹ 180   D) ₹ 200

18. **How much less does one pair of sandals costs than two shirts?**

   A) ₹ 100   B) ₹ 120   C) ₹ 150   D) ₹ 300

19. **1 hr 10 mins before 5 p.m is____.**

   A) 3:50 p.m.   B) 4:00 p.m.   C) 4:10 p.m.   D) 4:50 p.m.

20. **At 8:45 p.m, the hour hand of the clock will be near to _____.**

   A) 7   B) 8   C) 9   D) Cannot say

EVERYDAY MATHEMATICS

21. **Anita reached the market at 10:40 a.m, She shopped there for 1 hr and 10 mins and then she left the market, At what time did she leave the market?**

A) 11:45 a.m.   B) 12:00 p.m.   C) 11:50 a.m.   D) 11:40 a.m.

22. **Amit got the amount shown as his birthday gift. Which of the follwong options is CORRECT with respect to the amount of money shown here?**

A) 100 + 50 + 5

B) One hundred fifty seven

C) 100 ones + 50 ones + 2 ones

D) One hundred + 5 ones

23. **Sadhana started driving at 7:30 p.m. She reached her destination at 9:45 p.m. How long did she drive?**

A) 2 hrs

B) 1 hr 15 mins

C) 2 hrs 15 mins

D) 1 hr 50 mins

24. **Sheela has ₹ 600. She purchased the following items. How much money is left with her after shopping?**

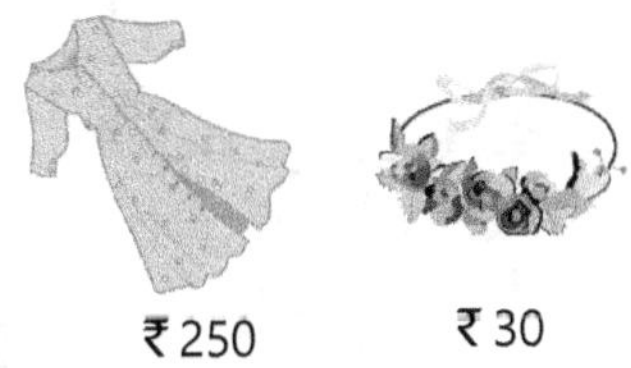

₹ 250   ₹ 30

A) ₹ 330   B) ₹ 320   C) ₹ 350   D) ₹ 250

25. **Anu takes 20 minutes to complete one round of the ground. How will she take to complete 3 rounds?**

A) 30 mins   B) 40 mins   C) 20 mins   D) 1 hr

ACHIVERS SECTION (HOTS)

26. **Read the given table and find the values of P, Q, R and S respectively.**

You are given	You are buying	Change received
	₹ 110	$P - Q = R$
	₹ 120	$P - 120 = S$

A) ₹ 110, ₹ 40, ₹ 150, ₹ 30   B) ₹ 150, ₹ 110, ₹ 40, ₹ 30

C) ₹ 30, ₹ 40, ₹ 110, ₹ 150   D) ₹ 110, ₹ 40, ₹ 150, ₹ 30

27. **Amit, Amol, Sushant and Sandeep leave their respective homes at 5:30 p.m for playing in the park. Amit reaches to the park at 5:45 p.m, Amol reaches at 5:40 p.m, Sushant reaches at 5:50 p.m and Sandeep reaches at 5:39 p.m. Who reaches earliest to the park and who reaches last respectively?**

A) Sandeep, Sushant   B) Amit, Sandeep

C) Sushant, Sandeep   D) Amol, Amit

28. **Ronak spends ₹ 370 to buy two of the following items. Which two things did he buy?**

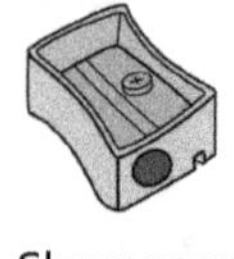  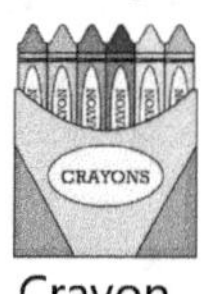  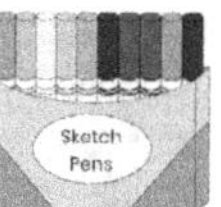

Sharpener	Cricket bat	Crayon	Shoes	Sketch pen
₹ 5	₹ 150	₹ 75	₹ 220	₹ 100

A) Sketch pen and Crayon   B) Sketch pen and Cricket bat

C) Sketch pen and Shoes   D) Cricket bat and Shoes

29. **Meena buys one cosliest item and one cheapest item. If she gives a ₹ 100 note to the seller, then how much money will she get back from the seller?**

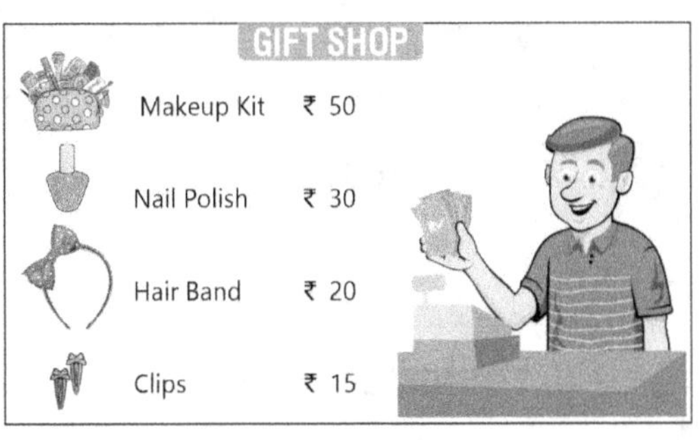

A) ₹ 40   B) ₹ 35   C) ₹ 30   D) ₹ 50

30. **Rohit starts his cricket practice on 1st July 20XX. If every Sunday is a holiday and he practices regularly for 15 days, then his practice finishes on____.**

July 20XX						
Mon	Tue	Wed	Thu	Fri	Sat	Sun
			1	2	3	4
5	6	7	8	9	10	11
12	13	14	15	16	17	18
19	20	21	22	23	24	25
26	27	28	29	30	31	

A) Friday   B) Sunday   C) Thursday   D) Saturday

Colour your choice with color pencil				
1	**2**	**3**	**4**	**5**
A B C D	A B C D	A B C D	A B C D	A B C D
6	**7**	**8**	**9**	**10**
A B C D	A B C D	A B C D	A B C D	A B C D
11	**12**	**13**	**14**	**15**
A B C D	A B C D	A B C D	A B C D	A B C D
16	**17**	**18**	**19**	**20**
A B C D	A B C D	A B C D	A B C D	A B C D
21	**22**	**23**	**24**	**25**
A B C D	A B C D	A B C D	A B C D	A B C D

LINES, SHAPES AND SOLIDS

* Identification of shapes and solids with their names.
* Counting of number of shapes, solids, slanting lines, sleeping lines, curved lines, straight lines, vertical lines, horizontal lines in geometrical figures
* Number of corners, sides and faces of geometrical figures
* Identification of shapes usesd to form solids

MATHEMATICAL REASONING

1. How many triangles are there in the given figure?

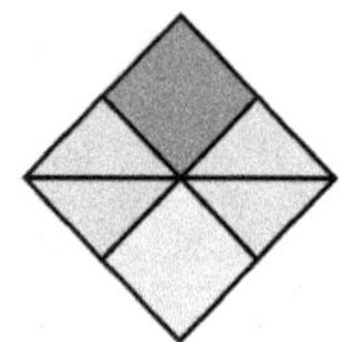

   A) 4   B) 5

   C) 6   D) 8

2. How many curved lines does the given figure has?

   A) 4   B) 5

   C) 3   D) 8

3. Which of the following shape is missing in the given figure?

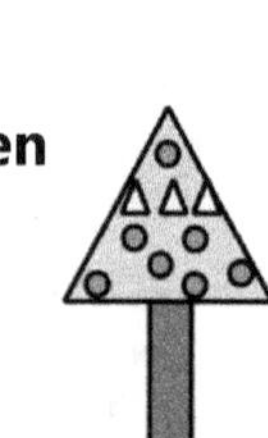

   A) Rectangle   B) Triangle

   C) Circle   D) Square

4. How many triangles are there in the given figure?

   A) 8

B) 10

C) 3

D) 5

5. **How many straight lines are there in the given figure?.**

   A) 11   B) 10

   C) 7   D) 8

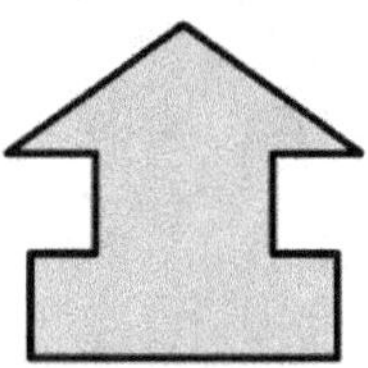

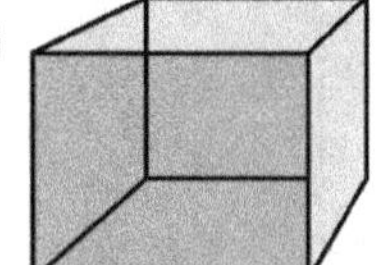

6. **How many flat faces are there in the given figure?**

   A) 6   B) 5

   C) 4   D) 7

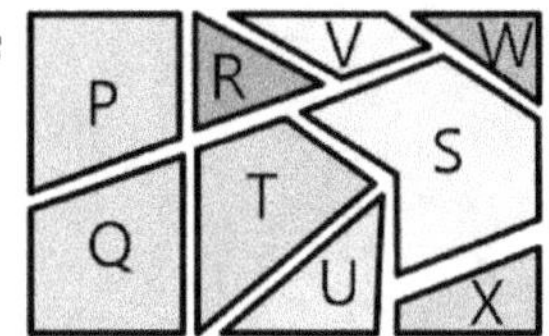

7. **Shape____ has the largest number of sides.**

   A) P   B) T

   C) S   D) R

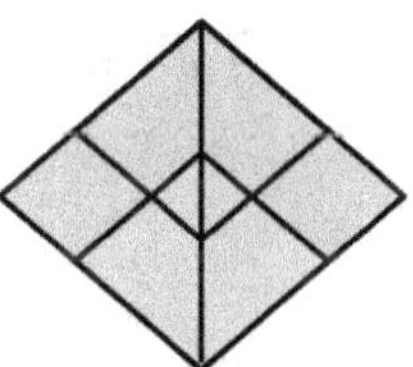

8. **How many straight lines are required to form the given figure?**

   A) 9   B) 13

   C) 10   D) 12

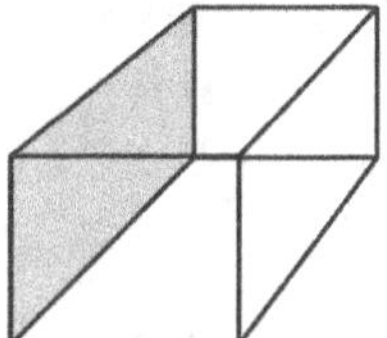

9. **Identify the shape of the shaded face of the given solid.**

   A) Circle   B) Rectangle

   C) Square   D) Triangle

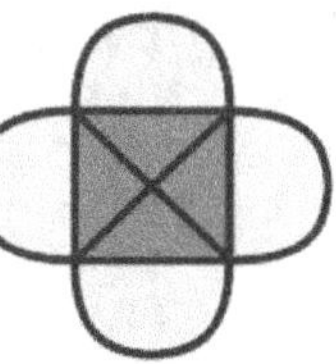

10. **Given figure is formed by ____ curved lines and 6 straight lines.**

    A) 4   B) 5   C) 6   D) 3

11. **How many curved lines are there in the given figure?**

    A) 4   B) 5

    C) 3   D) 2

12. **How many squares are there in the given figure?**

    A) 7

    B) 10

    C) 11

    D) 4

13. **Which of the following shape is missing in the given figure?**

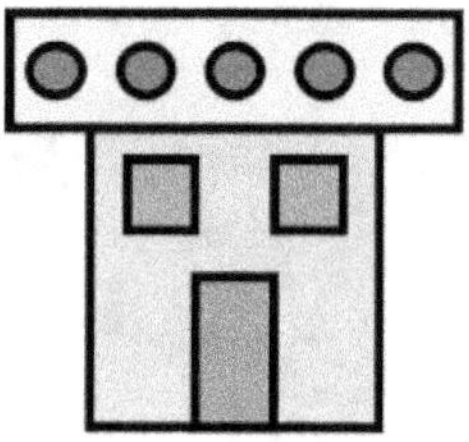

    A) 'Rectangle

    B) Square

    C) Triangle

    D) Circle

14. **Number of slanting lines in the given figures is ___**

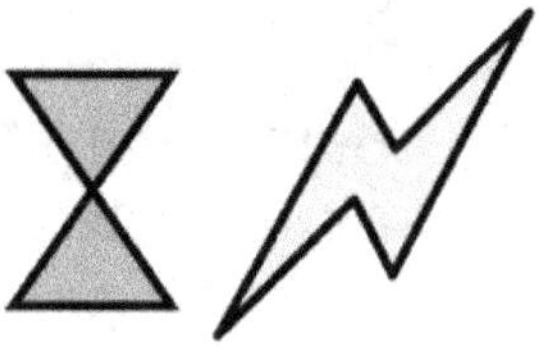

    A) 6   B) 8

    C) 10   D) 4

15. **How many ⬭ are there in the given figure?**

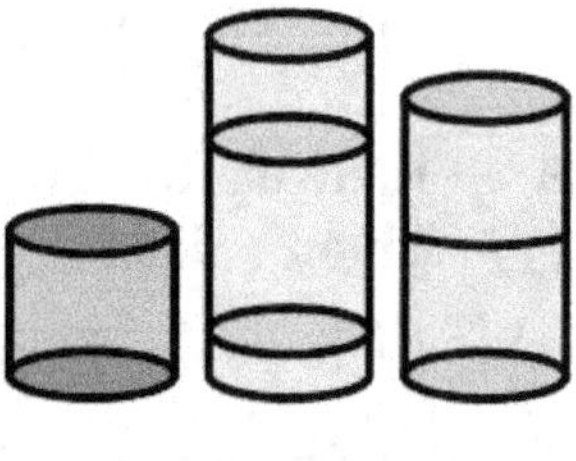

    A) 7   B) 9

    C) 6   D) 5

16. **How many squares are there in the given shape?**

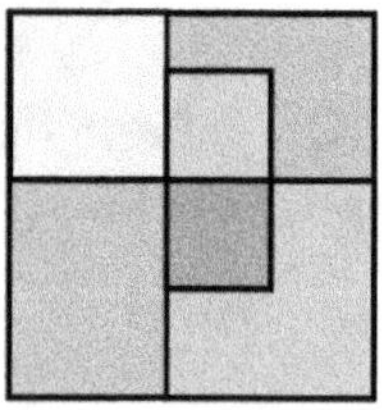

    A) 7   B) 5

    C) 8   D) 6

17. The number of sleeping lines in the given figures is ____

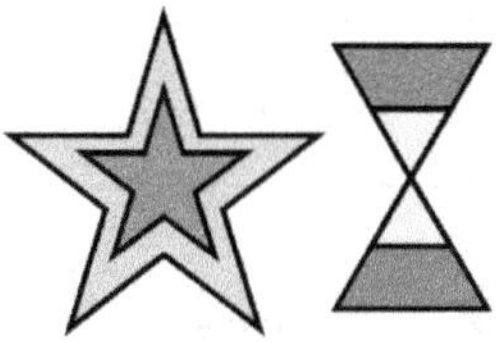

A) 4   B) 6

C) 8   D) 10

18. The number of straight lines needed to make the given figure are ____

A) 6   B) 12

C) 8   D) 10

19. The given figure has ____ curved lines and ____ straight lines.

A) 2, 2   B) 3, 2

C) 1, 2   D) 2, 3

20. The given figures has ____ curved lines.

A) 6   B) 4

C) 5   D) 7

EVERYDAY MATHEMATICS

21. Priyanka has some stickers.

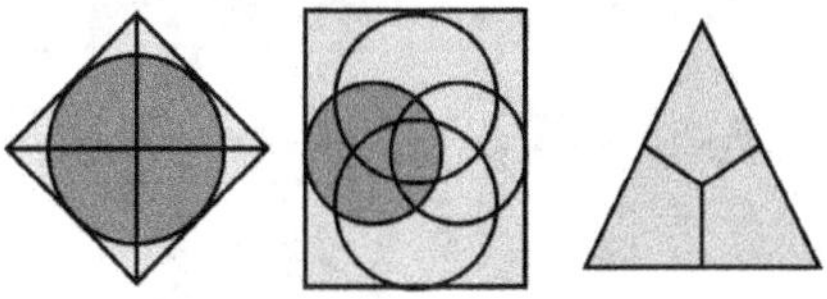

There are ____ circles in the stickers altogther.

A) 3   B) 5   C) 4   D) 6

22. Sonali has 8 matchsticks of same size. She made a figure using the matchsticks so that it has 6 slanting and 2 sleeping lines. Which of the following can be her picture?

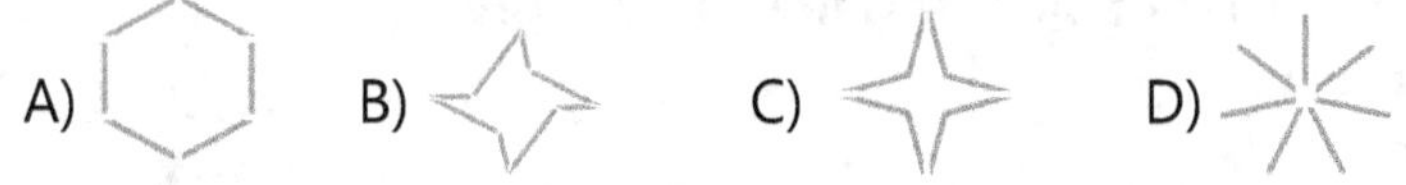

A)   B)   C)   D)

23. **Divya is trying to make a triangle using straws and balls of clay. She uses straws of making edges and clay balls for making corners. How many straws and balls of clay will she need?**

A) 3 straws, 3 balls of clay   B) 3 straws, 2 balls of clay
C) 4 straws, 4 balls of clay   D) 6 straws, 4 balls of clay

24. **Arun saw the following flag in the school annual games.**

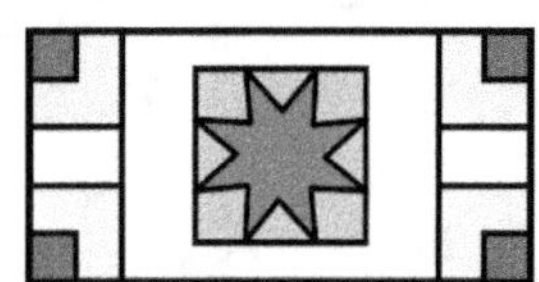

How many squares did Arun see?

A) 8   B) 7   C) 9   D) 11

25. **If Poonam places 10 matchbox one above the another, then which of the given shapes will she get?**

A) Triangle   B) Rectangle   C) Square   D) Cylinder

ACHIVERS SECTION (HOTS)

26. **Which of the following has the minimum number of unit squares?**

1 ☐ = 1 unit square

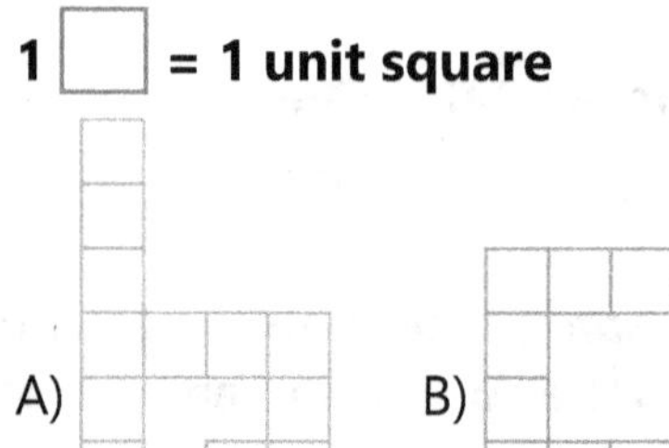

A)

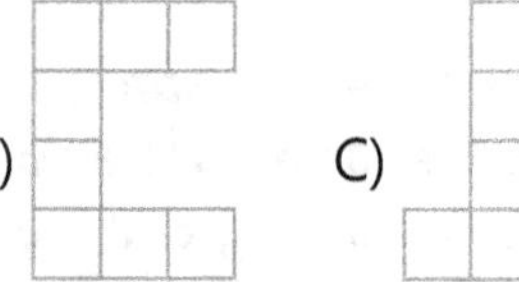

B)

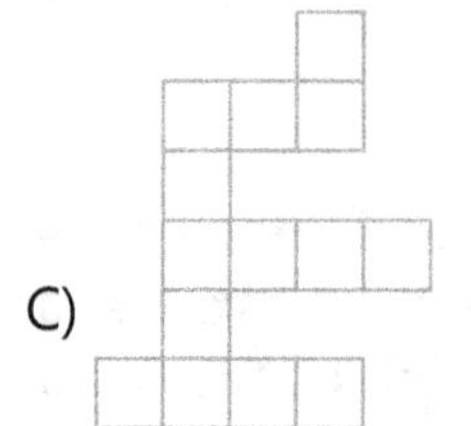

C)

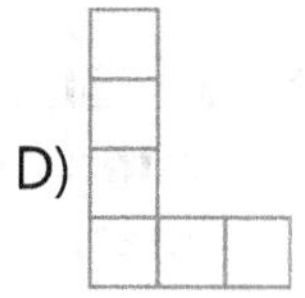

D)

27. Complete the figures given in column-1 with their missing parts given in column-2.

1.    A) 

2.    B) 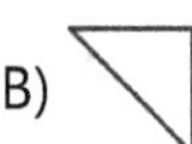

3.    C) ☐

4. 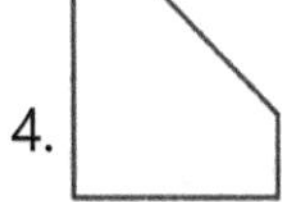   D) △

A) 1 → (D), 2 → (C), 3 → (B), 4 → (A)

B) 1 → (D), 2 → (B), 3 → (A), 4 → (C)

C) 1 → (C), 2 → (D), 3 → (B), 4 → (A)

D) 1 → (C), 2→ (D), 3 → (A), 4 → (B)

28. The given figures has ___ standing lines and ____ sleeping lines.

A) 4, 2   B) 4, 6

C) 2, 6   D) 6, 4

29. Manisha and her friend have some shapes given below.

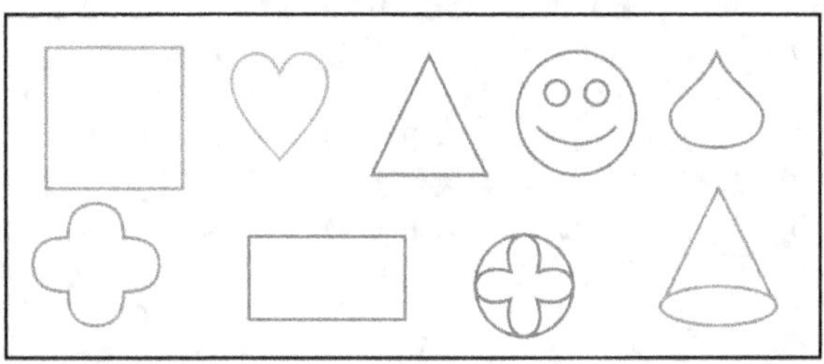

Manisha thought of the shapes that are similar in a certain way as follows:

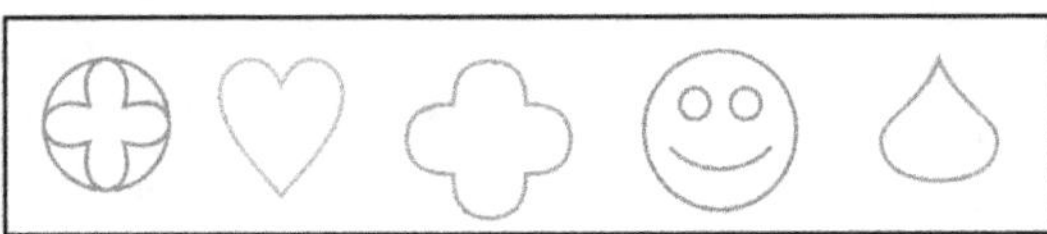

On what basis did alisha distinguish the given shapes?

A) The shapes are made up more than four sides.

B) The shapes are made up only curved lines.

C) The shapes are made up of only straight lines

D) The shapes are made up of only four sides.

30. **The given figure is made up of _____ triangles,___ squares and ____rectangle.**

A) 2, 4, 1

B) 4, 2, 1

C) 2, 2, 1

D) 4, 4, 1

Colour your choice with color pencil				
1	**2**	**3**	**4**	**5**
A B C D	A B C D	A B C D	A B C D	A B C D
6	**7**	**8**	**9**	**10**
A B C D	A B C D	A B C D	A B C D	A B C D
11	**12**	**13**	**14**	**15**
A B C D	A B C D	A B C D	A B C D	A B C D
16	**17**	**18**	**19**	**20**
A B C D	A B C D	A B C D	A B C D	A B C D
21	**22**	**23**	**24**	**25**
A B C D	A B C D	A B C D	A B C D	A B C D

PATTERNS

* Finding the next term/next figure in the number pattern/figure pattern.
* Finding the missing term/figure in the number pattern/figure pattern.

DIRECTION (1-15): Complete the number pattern in the following questions.

1. **15, 19, 23____31, 35.**

   A) 27   B) 28   C) 31   D) 35

2. **22, 33, 44, 55, 66____**

   A) 75   B) 77   C) 72   D) 71

3. **14, 28, 42, 56, 70____**

   A) 84   B) 82   C) 84   D) 88

4. **10, 20, 35, 55, 80____**

   A) 110   B) 90   C) 115   D) 120

5. **50, 150, 250, 350, 450 ____**

   A) 555   B) 551   C) 550   D) 455

6. **6, 11, 16, 21 ______**

   A) 23   B) 26   C) 28   D) 25

7. **110, 115, 125, 130, 140, 145 _____**

   A) 140   B) 150   C) 155   D) 165

8. **500, 520, 540, 560, 580 _____**

A) 610 B) 655 C) 600 D) 590

9. 527, 530, 533, 536 _____

A) 534 B) 538 C) 539 D) 535

10. 220, 215, 205, 200, 190 _____

A) 185 B) 195 C) 190 D) 180

11. _______ 200, 185, 170, 155

A) 213 B) 210 C) 215 D) 200

12. 125, _____ 325, 425, 525, 625

A) 248 B) 225 C) 126 D) 138

13. 8, 16, 24, 32, 40 ______

A) 41 B) 42 C) 44 D) 48

14. 115, 125, 135 _____ 155, 165 _____185, 195

A) 145, 175 B) 140, 170 C) 175, 145 D) 136, 162

15. 80, 70, 61, 53 ____ 40, 35

A) 43 B) 50 C) 48 D) 46

DIRECTION (16-30) : Find the missing figure to complete the given figure pattern

16. 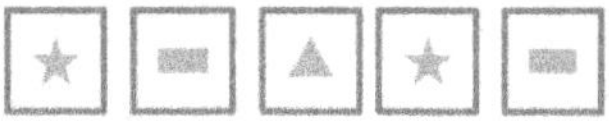 _____

A) 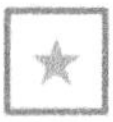 B) C) 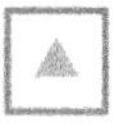 D) 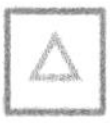

17. 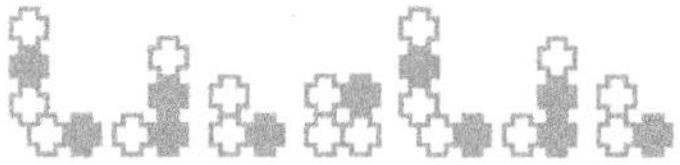 _____ 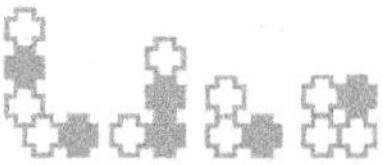

A) B) C) 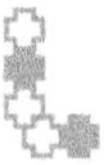 D) 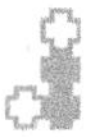

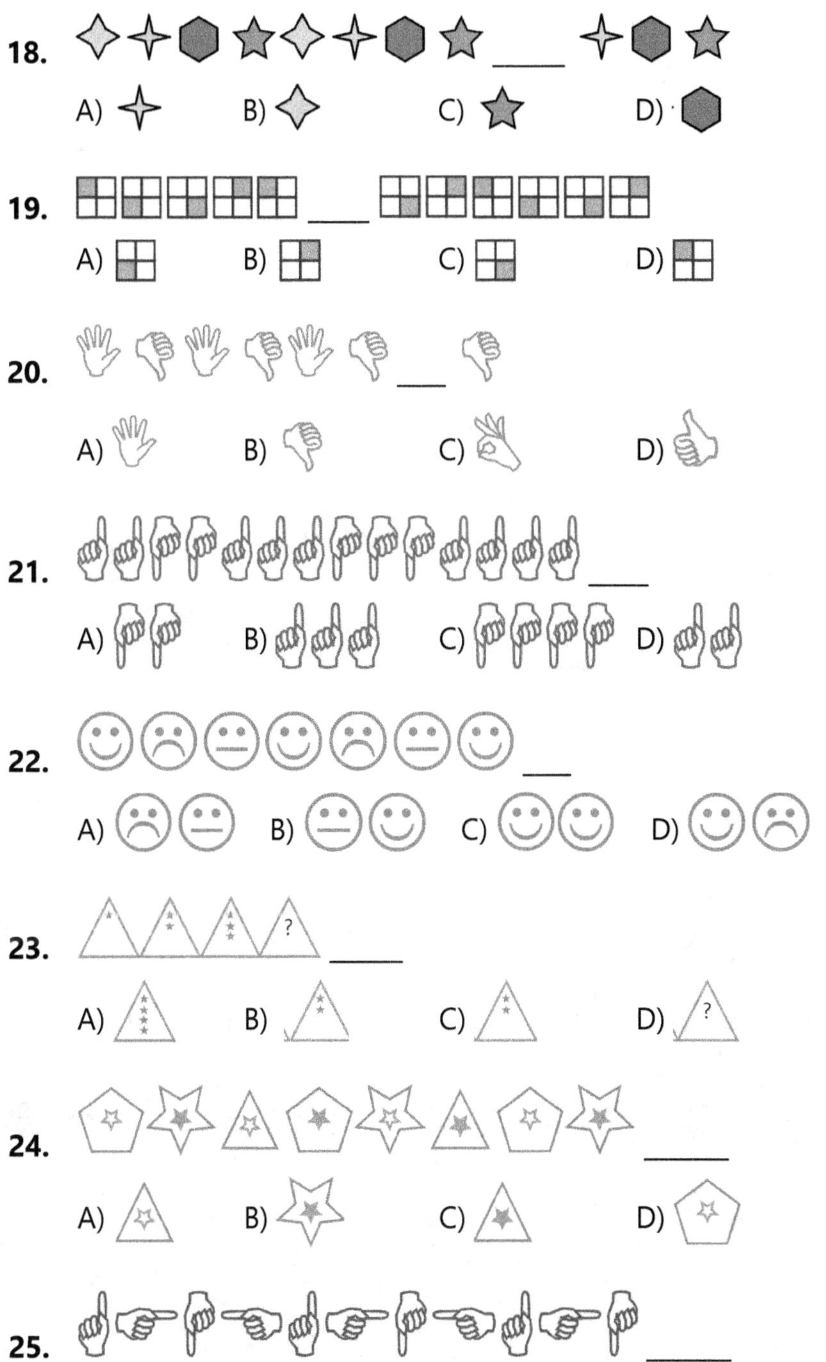

A) 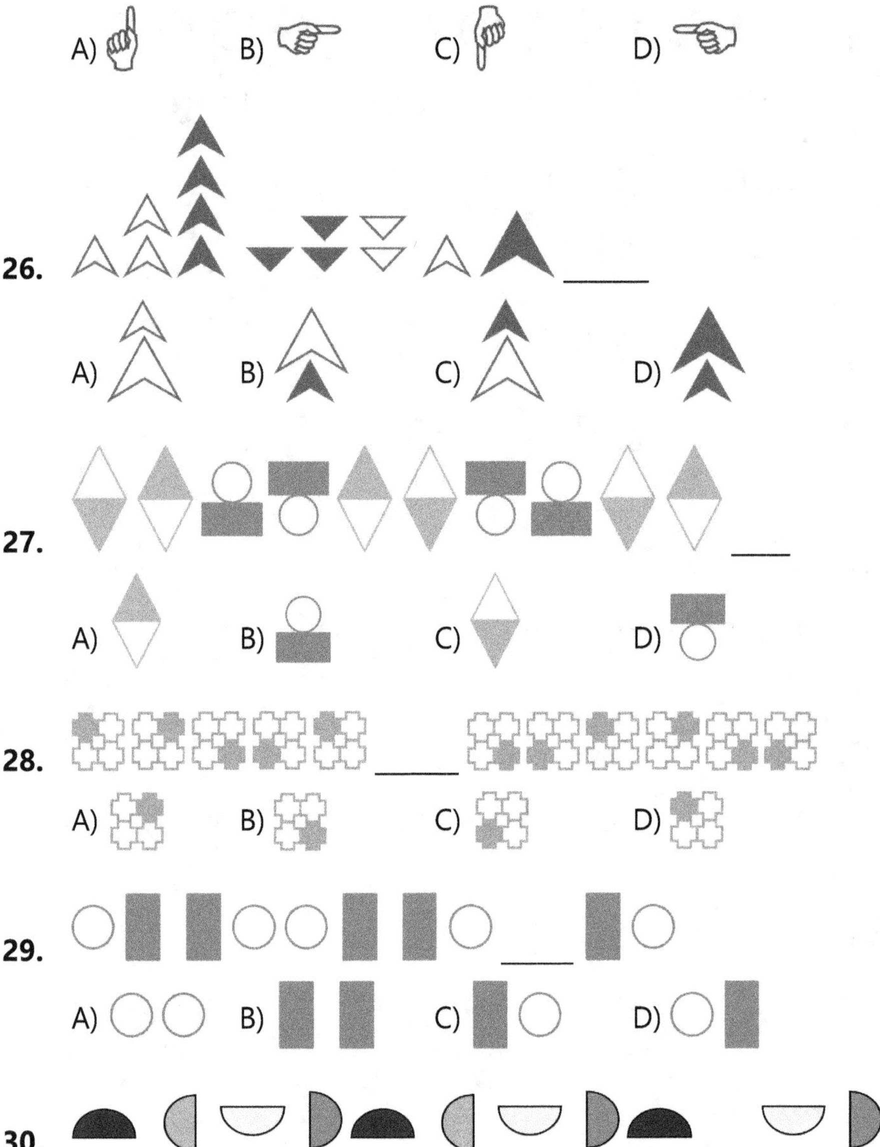

26.

A)   B)   C)   D)

27.

A)   B)   C)   D)

28.

A)   B)   C)   D)

29.

A)   B)   C)   D)

30.

A)   B)   C)   D)

PICTOGRAPHS

* Answer the questions based on the data in pictograph/picture graph.

MATHEMATICAL REASONING

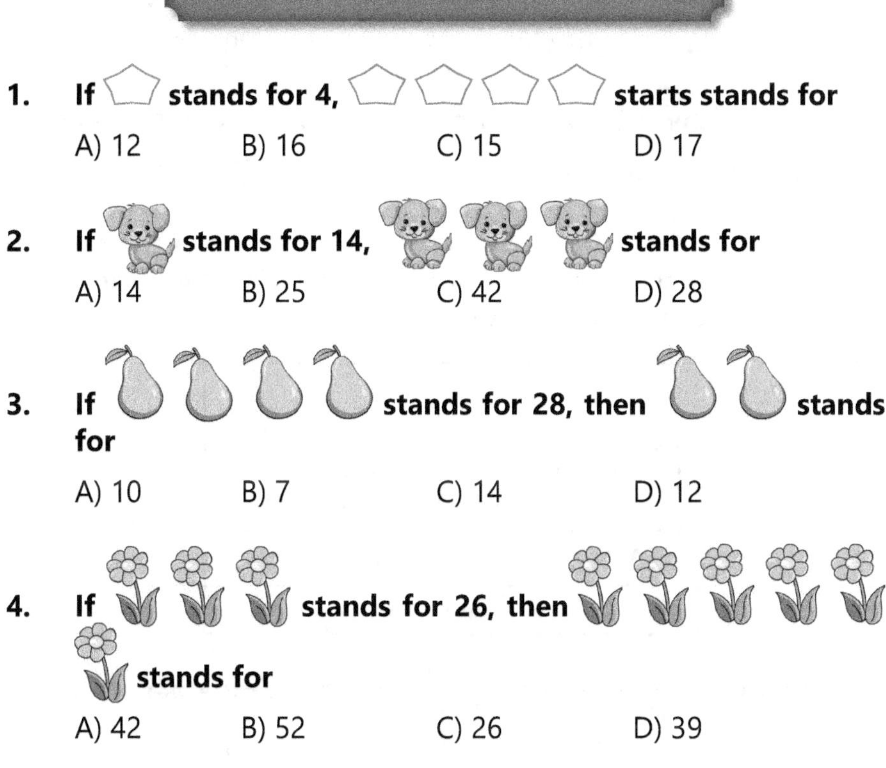

1. If ⬠ stands for 4, ⬠⬠⬠⬠ starts stands for

   A) 12   B) 16   C) 15   D) 17

2. If 🐶 stands for 14, 🐶🐶🐶 stands for

   A) 14   B) 25   C) 42   D) 28

3. If 🍐🍐🍐🍐 stands for 28, then 🍐🍐 stands for

   A) 10   B) 7   C) 14   D) 12

4. If 🌼🌼🌼 stands for 26, then 🌼🌼🌼🌼🌼🌼 stands for

   A) 42   B) 52   C) 26   D) 39

DIRECTION (5-7): The given pictograph shows the number of students in each section of class 4. Study the graph and answer the following questions.

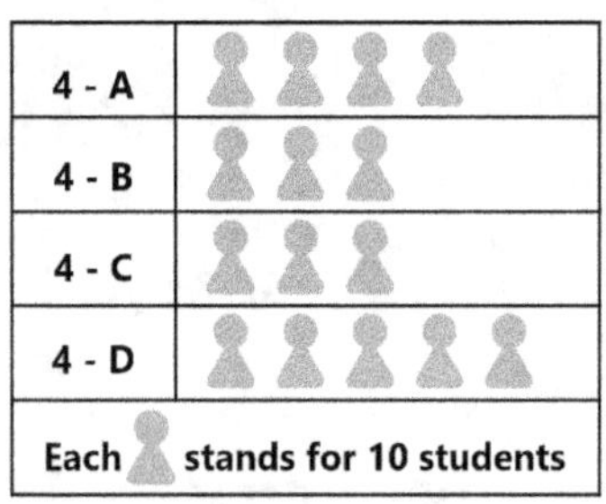

5 **Maximum number of students are in ___**

A) 4 - A   B) 4 - B   C) 4 - C   D) 4 - D

6. **Which two sections has same number of students?**

A) 4 - A, 4 - B   B) 4 - D, 4 - B   C) 4 - C, 4 - B   D) 4 - A, 4 - C

7. **How many total number of students are there in class 4?**

A) 150   B) 100   C) 120   D) 180

DIRECTION: (8-9): The given pictograph shows the number of braceletes beaded by 4 different girls. Study the graph answer the following question.

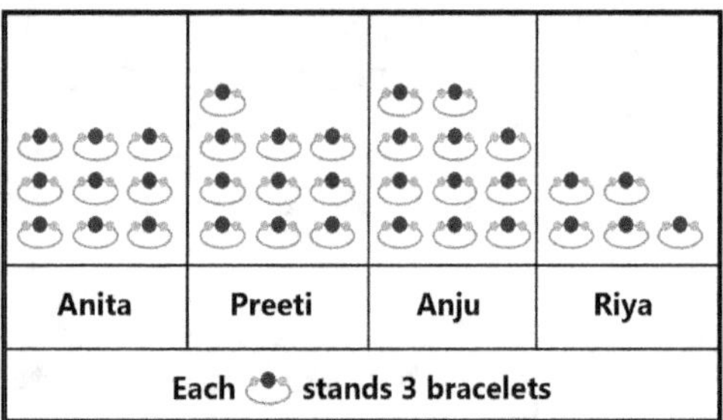

8. **Anita and Anju beaded ____ braceletes altogether.**

A) 60   B) 30   C) 50   D) 40

9. **Riya beaded___fewer braceletes than Preeti.**

A) 18   B) 20   C) 15   D) 10

DIRECTION (10-11): The given picture graph shows the

various types of books some students like for vacation. Study the graph and answer the given questions.

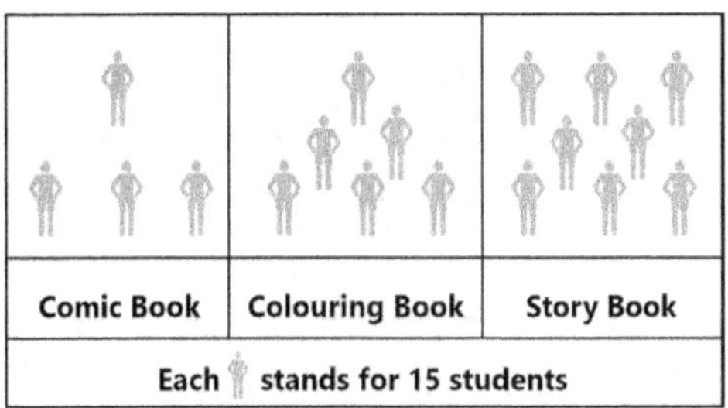

10. Most boys prefer___

A) Comic book

B) Colouring book

C) Story book

D) Can't be determined

11. ___ more boys prefer colouring books than comic books.

A) 30 B) 15 C) 20 D) 10

DIRECTION (12-14): The given pictograph shows the number of trophy stickers achieved by five children in a month. Study the graph and answer the given question.

Anil	🏆 🏆
Ansh	🏆 🏆 🏆
Jay	🏆
Minal	🏆 🏆 🏆 🏆 🏆
Monika	🏆 🏆
Each 🏆 stands for 2 trophies	

12. Who got minimum trophies ?

A) Jay B) Monika C) Minal D) Ansh

13. Which two children got same number of trophies ?

A) Minal and Anil

B) Anil and Monika

C) Anil and Jay

D) Minal and Ansh

14. **Minal got _______ more trophies than Ansh.**

A) 8   B) 2   C) 4   D) 6

DIRECTION (15-17): The given picture graph shows the number of television Mr. Warma sold in 4 different months. Study the graph carefully and answer the following questions.

February	🖵 🖵 🖵 🖵
March	🖵 🖵 🖵
April	🖵 🖵
May	🖵 🖵 🖵 🖵 🖵
Each 🖵 stands for 15 television	

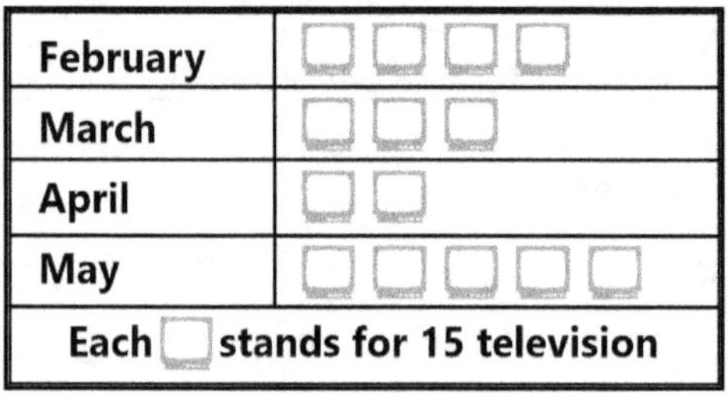

15. **How many televisions did Mr. Warma sold in March?**

A) 45   B) 40   C) 30   D) 35

16. **In which month least number of televisions were sold?**

A) April   B) March   C) February   D) May

17. **How many more televisions were sold in May than in April?**

A) 40   B) 70   C) 45   D) 60

DIRECTION (18-20): The given picture graphs shows the types of colours various girls prefer. Study the graph and answer the following questions.

Pink	Yellow	Orange	Maroon
★★★★★★ ★★★★ ★★★★	★★★★★ ★★★★ ★★★★	★★★★ ★★★★ ★★★★	★★★★ ★★★★
Each ★ stands 2 girls			

18. **How many more girls prefer pink than yellow colour?**

A) 10   B) 6   C) 8   D) 11

19. **Which colour is least liked by girls?**

   A) Maroon   B) Yellow   C) Pink   D) Orange

20. **How many girls prefer Orange and Maroon colour altogther?**

   A) 40   B) 24   C) 40   D) 30

DIRECTION (21-22): The given pictogrph shows the number of toys sold by a leading toy store in 4 different months. Study the graph and answer the following questions.

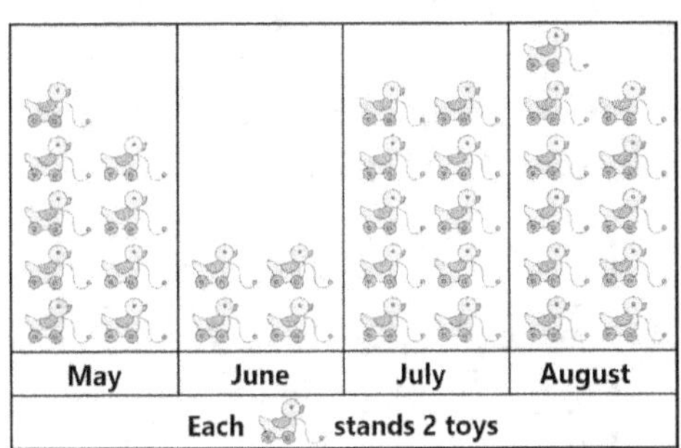

21. **How many toys were sold in four months altogther?**

   A) 92   B) 34   C) 70   D) 68

22. **How many more toys were sold in May than in June?**

   A) 7   B) 20   C) 25   D) 10

DIRECTION: (23-25): The given picture graph shows the various types of sports that children prefer. Study the graph and answer the follwing questions.

Cricket	🖐🖐🖐🖐🖐🖐🖐
Badminton	🖐🖐🖐🖐
Swimming	🖐🖐🖐
Cycling	🖐🖐🖐🖐🖐🖐
Each 🖐 stands for 4 children	

23. **How many children prefer playing badminton?**

A) 24　　　　B) 25　　　　C) 20　　　　D) 15

24. **Which type of sports is most popular ?**

　　A) Cricket　　B) Badminton　C) Swimming　D) Cycling

25. **How many more children prefer cycling than swimming**

　　A) 15　　　　B) 11　　　　C) 18　　　　D) 12

ACHIVERS SECTION (HOTS)

26. **The given picture graph shows the number of burgers Varun sold from Monday to Thursday.**

Monday	🍔 🍔 🍔 🍔
Tuesday	🍔
Wednesday	🍔 🍔
Thursday	🍔 🍔 🍔

Each 🍔 stands for 10 burgers

　　If Varun sold each burger for ₹ 2. How much more money did he collect on Thursday then on Wednesday

　　A) ₹ 80　　B) ₹ 20　　　C) ₹ 50　　　D) ₹ 40

27. **Kavita needs some chart paper to complete her school project. She bought 12 green coloured papers, 15 blue coloured papers, 9 yellow coloured papers and 18 red coloured papers.**

　　If each paper = 3 papers, then which of the following pictograph is correct?

A)

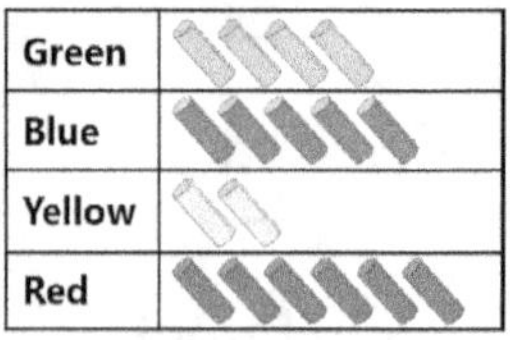

Green	
Blue	
Yellow	
Red	

B)

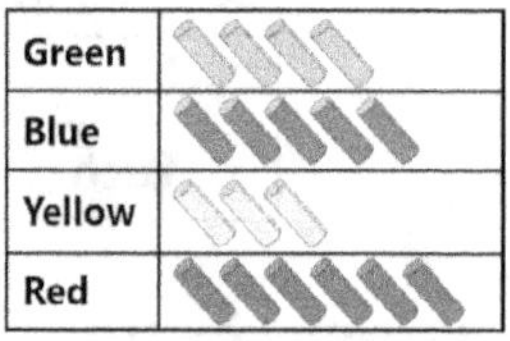

Green	
Blue	
Yellow	
Red	

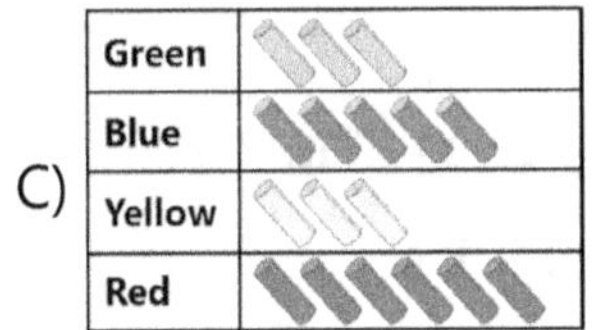

Green	(3 bars)
Blue	(4 bars)
Yellow	(3 bars)
Red	(6 bars)

C) (table above)

D) None of these

28. The given picture graph shows the number of students for the events at a sports meet.

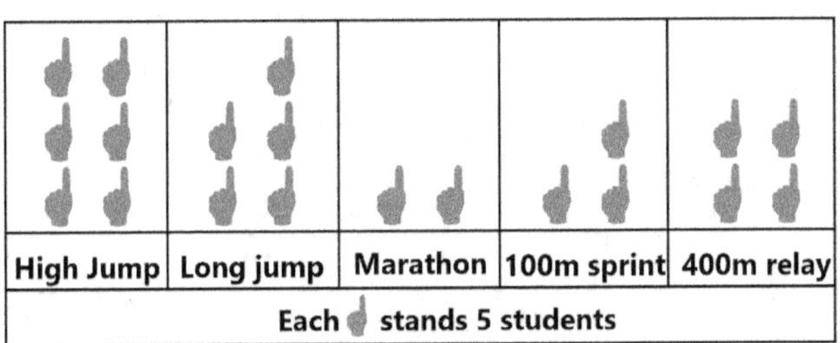

The number of participants for which event is the same as the total number of participants for marathon and 400 m relay?

A) High jump   B) Long jump   C) 100 m sprint   D) 400 m relay

29. The following pictograph shows the number of trees planted by some students.

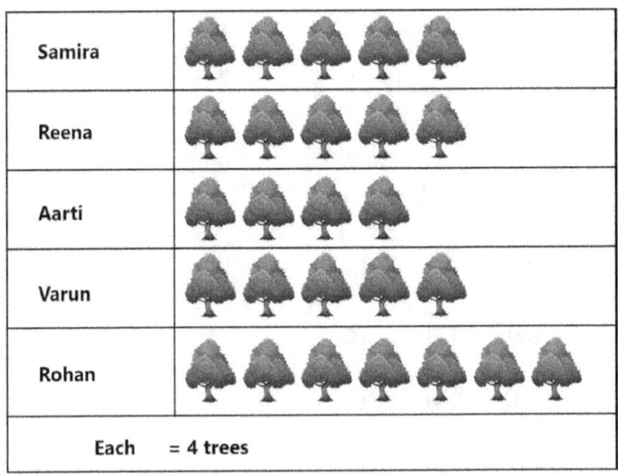

Using the given information, find out which of the following statements is CORRECT ?

A) Rohan planted least number of trees.

B) Samira planted more numbers of trees than Varun.

C) Aarti planted the most number of trees.

D) Reena planted 20 trees.

30. Four children collected some pictue cards.

Match the name of children given in column 1 with their collected number of cards given in column

Column 1	Column 2
Sneha	(a) 250
Sanjeevani	(b) 200
Lata	(c) 300
Usha	(d) 400

	1	2	3	4
A)	(d)	(a)	(c)	(b)
B)	(c)	(d)	(a)	(b)
C)	(b)	(c)	(d)	(a)
D)	(c)	(a)	(d)	(b)

LOGICAL REASONING

* Number pattern/figure pattern
* Measuring length, weight, capacity, money, time and temperature
* Finding the missing figure in the first/second pair of figures using relation given in first/second pair of figure
* Completing the numbers matrix/figure by identifying the rule
* Counting the geometrical shapes/solids in figure
* Odd one out
* Embedded figures
* Ranking test
* Coding - Decoding
* Grouping of figures

MATHEMATICAL REASONING

1. Look at the given pattern.

How would you show this pattern using letters?

A) xxooxxooxxx

B) ooxxooxxoxxo

C) oooxooxooxooo

D) ooooxxoooxxx

2. How many shapes has the number of sides equal to 4?

A) 3

B) 5

C) 4

D) 8

3. **Rajan starts his maths exam practice from 1st August 20XX, If he practice for 15 days (and all Sundays are holidays), then his practice finishes on ___**

	August 20XX					
Mon	Tue	Wed	Thu	Fri	Sat	Sun
				1	2	3
4	5	6	7	8	9	10
11	12	13	14	15	16	17
18	19	20	21	22	23	24
25	26	27	28	29	30	31

A) Friday   B) Thursday

C) Monday   D) Saturday

4. **Find the kite from the options which is exactly same as the given kite.**

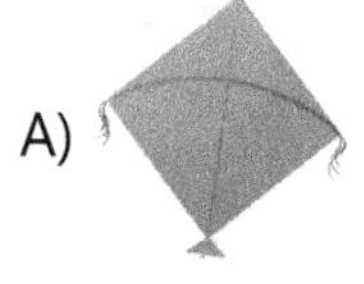

A)

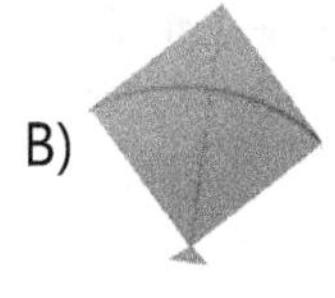

B)

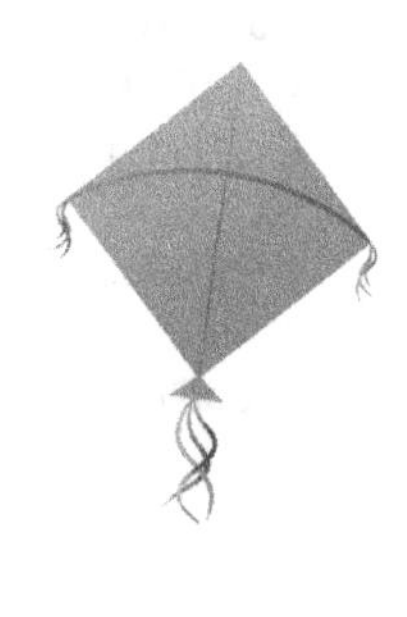

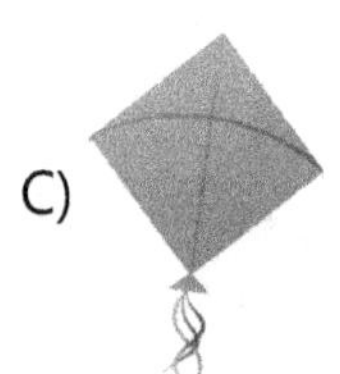

C)

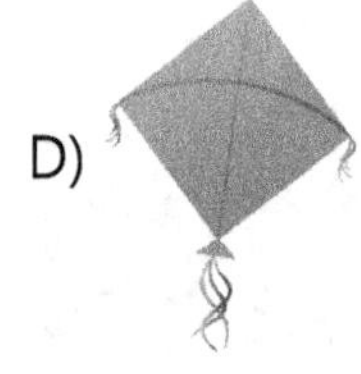

D)

5. **Which counting toy has the least number of rings?**

A) P

B) S

C) Q

D) R

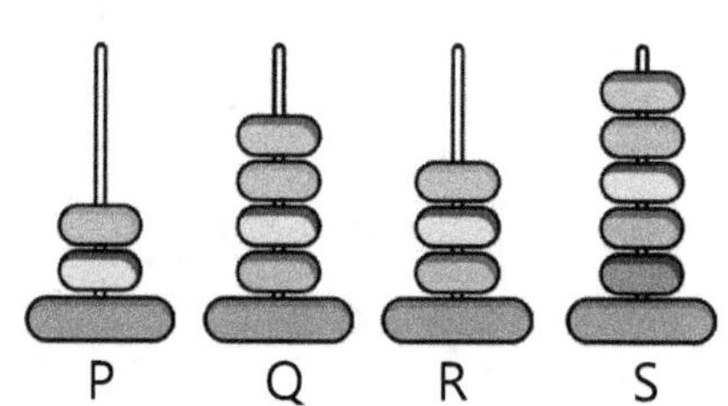

6. **Arrange the blocks from the heaviest to the lightest.**

A) P, S, Q, R   B) S, P, Q, R   C) R, Q, P, S   D) S, P, R, Q

7. **If Raju rotates the wheel, which number is least likely to come?**

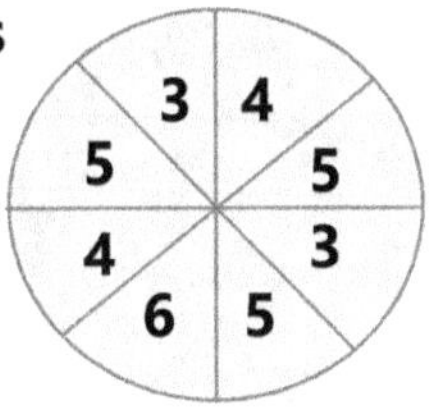

   A) 3   B) 4

   C) 5   D) 6

8. **If day before yesterday was Thursday then what day will be tomorrow?**

   A) Saturday   B) Friday   C) Tuesday   D) Sunday

9. **Which figure comes next in the figure pattern given below?**

   A)    B)    C)    D)

10. **Which alphabet is in the middle of the given word?**

    M A T H E M A T I C S

    A) H   B) A   C) M   D) E

11. **Rohit is shorter than Arun, Arun is shorter than Soham and Manthan is taller than Rohit but shorter than Arun. Who is the tallest among them?**

    A) Arun   B) Manthan   C) Rohit   D) Soham

12. **Find the odd one out.**

    A)    B)    C)    D)

13. **There are ___ more triangles than circles in the given figure.**

    A) 14   B) 23

    C) 18   D) 25

14. **Study the given picture carefully.**

Which of the following statements in INCORRECT ?

A) The toy duck is as heavy as the toy car.

B) The toy duck is lighter than the toy car.

C) The toy car is heavier than the toy duck.

D) All of the these

15. **Find the missing number to continue the given number pattern.**

A) 45   B) 44   C) 42   D) 50

16. **Which of the following alphabet is embedded in the figure?**

A) M   B) H

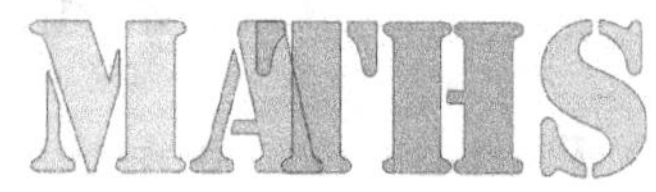

C) T   D) A

17. **If standing lines are called sleeping lines, sleeping lines are called curved lines and curved limes are slanting lines, then the square is formed by___**

A) Standing lines   B) Sleeping lines and curved lines

C) Curved lines   D) Slanting lines

18. **Which number is 4th to the right of 3rd number from the**

left end?

A) D   B) B   C) A   D) G

19. **The number of curved lines in the given figure is _____**

A) 6

B) 10

C) 7

D) 5

20. **Select the odd one out.**

A)    B)    C) 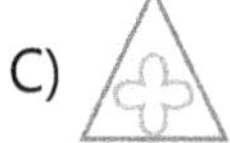   D) 

21. **Rohit needs to ride to Town Y via Town X for a school exam. The given figure shows the routes that he can take.**

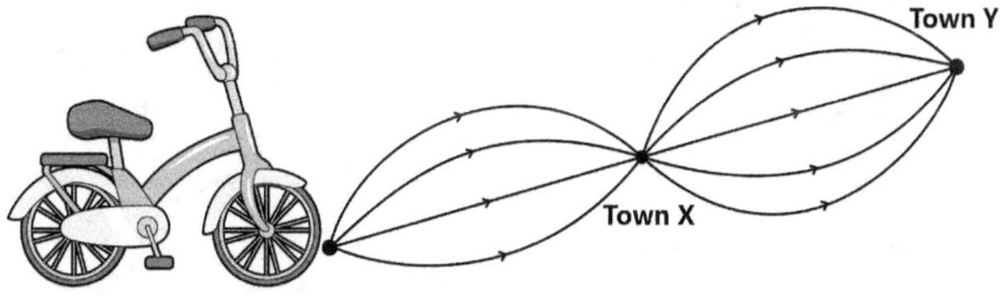

How many diffrent ways are there for Rohit to go town Y?

A) 15   B) 31   C) 20   D) 22

DIRECTION (22-23): There is a certain relationship between the pair of figures on the either side of: Identify the relation and find the missing figure.

22. 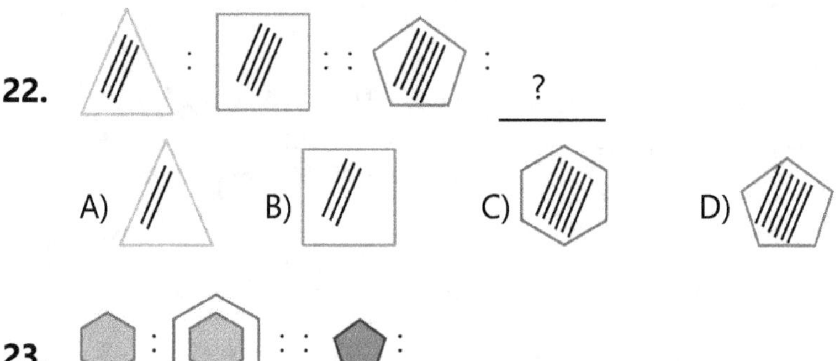

23. 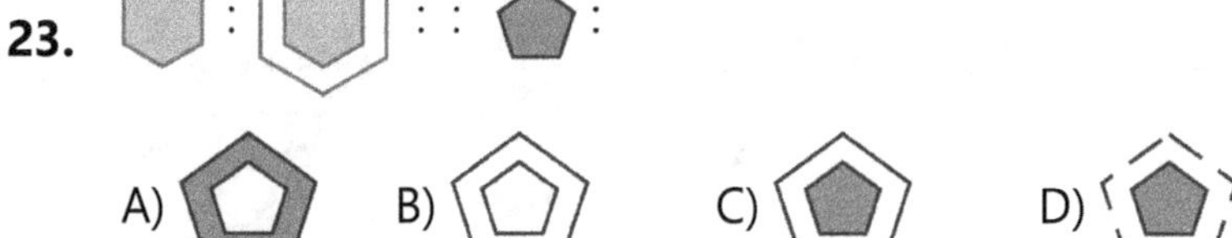

24. There are ___ equal groups of 12 grapes each.

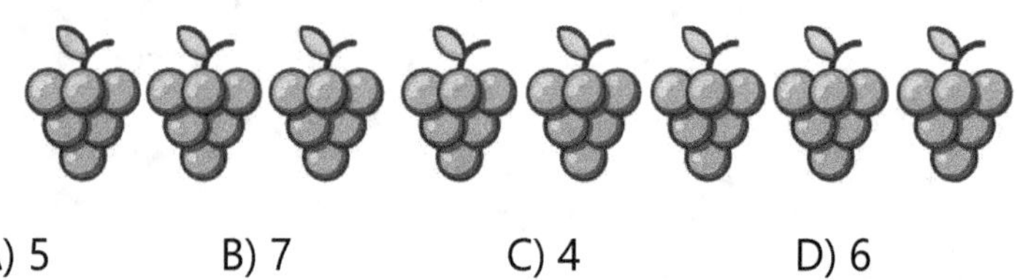

A) 5   B) 7   C) 4   D) 6

25. Which figure will complete the given pattern?

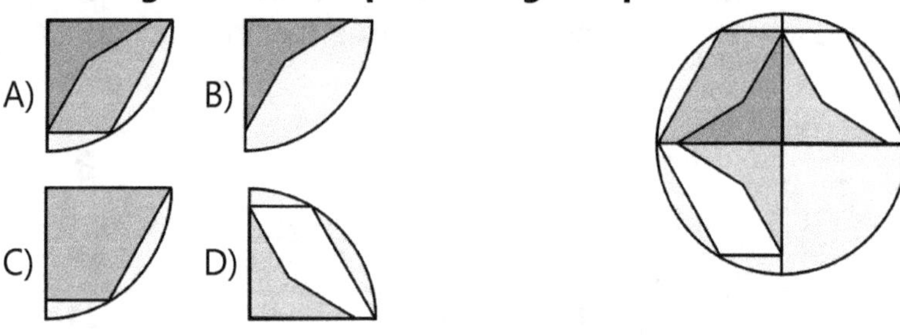

26. If the cycle is removed from the arrangement given below, then which item is fifth from the left end?

A) V   B) Q   C) R   D) U

27. If  means , 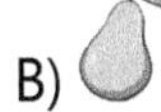 means and  means 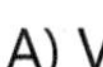 then which one is the king of fruits?

A)    B)   C)   D)

28. **Which of the following shapes is missing in the given figure?**

A) Triangle   B) Square

C) Circle   D) Rectangle

29. **How many groups of 5 candles each can be formed from the given candles?**

A) 5   B) 3   C) 4   D) 6

30. **Find the missing number.**

A) 18   B) 15

C) 19   D) 11

$$3 \quad \boxed{24} \quad 5 \qquad 2 \quad \boxed{20} \quad 10 \qquad 8 \quad \boxed{?} \quad 5$$
$$7 \qquad 9 \quad 5 \qquad 3 \qquad 2$$

<table>
<tr><td colspan="5" align="center">**Colour your choice with color pencil**</td></tr>
<tr><td align="center">1</td><td align="center">2</td><td align="center">3</td><td align="center">4</td><td align="center">5</td></tr>
<tr><td>A B C D</td><td>A B C D</td><td>A B C D</td><td>A B C D</td><td>A B C D</td></tr>
<tr><td align="center">6</td><td align="center">7</td><td align="center">8</td><td align="center">9</td><td align="center">10</td></tr>
<tr><td>A B C D</td><td>A B C D</td><td>A B C D</td><td>A B C D</td><td>A B C D</td></tr>
<tr><td align="center">11</td><td align="center">12</td><td align="center">13</td><td align="center">14</td><td align="center">15</td></tr>
<tr><td>A B C D</td><td>A B C D</td><td>A B C D</td><td>A B C D</td><td>A B C D</td></tr>
<tr><td align="center">16</td><td align="center">17</td><td align="center">18</td><td align="center">19</td><td align="center">20</td></tr>
<tr><td>A B C D</td><td>A B C D</td><td>A B C D</td><td>A B C D</td><td>A B C D</td></tr>
<tr><td align="center">21</td><td align="center">22</td><td align="center">23</td><td align="center">24</td><td align="center">25</td></tr>
<tr><td>A B C D</td><td>A B C D</td><td>A B C D</td><td>A B C D</td><td>A B C D</td></tr>
</table>

Hints & Explanations

1 Number Sense

1. (B) : The place value of digit 5 in 577 is 500 as 5 is at hundred's place.

2. (D) : Nine hundred seven = 907

3. (B) : The number more than 200 but less than 500 present on the box is 390

4. (B) : The sheet which shows 3 stars at hundred's place 4 stars at ten's place and 7 star's at one's place is the sheet showing 347.

5. (B) : 259 is the largest 3-digit odd number

6. (C) : Ascending order of given numbers is 114, 198, 255, 314, 422.

    So, the second smallest number in the group is 198

7. (B) : Two hundred seventy one, i.e., 271 belong to the given collection of numbers

8. (C) : 80 tens = 800

    9 hundreds = 900

    Hence, 80 tens is less than 900

9. (B) : In numbers five hundred and seven is written as 507.

10. (A) : Largest 3-digit number is 999

11. (C) : The smallest number amongst the numbers is 717.

12. (B) : 40 tens = 400 and 550 is more than 400.

    Hence, option (B) is correct

13. (A) : Five hundred fifty five is written as 55.

14. (A) : Smallest 3-digit number is 100

15. (C) : Nine hundreds and nine in numbers is written as 909.

16. (D) : Option (D) is correct because Two hundred and twelve is written as 212.

17. (C) : Kite P shows 80 tens = 800

    Kite P shows 80 tens = 800

    Kite Q shows 50 ones = 50

    Kite R shows 70 ones = 70

    Kite S shows 20 ones = 20

    So kite S shows the smallest value.

18. (A) : Decreasing order of given numbers is 590, 579, 552, 53533

19. (A) : In 561 , the digit 6 is at ten's place.

20. (B) :

21. (D) : Since 255 > 250. So, 255 cannot be the number of muffins baked by Simran.

22. (B) : The smallest possible 3-digit number formed by using the digits 5, 8, 2 is 258

23. (B) : The sheet formed by Radha will be

24. (D) : Number of toys Sayali has = 52 ones = 52

Number of toys Poonam has = 3 tens 8 ones = 250

Number of toys Shiv has = 8 tens 3 ones = 803

So, Sayali has maximum number of toys is an incorrect statement

25. (C) : Jacky ate 322 bananas

26. (C) : The place value of 9 is 947

27. (D) : 1. The largest 3-digit number is 999 and 2 less than 999 = 999 – 2 = 997.

2. 50 one = 50

3. Six hundred and twenty is same as 622

28. (B) : P. 5 hundreds + 2 ones = 500 + 2 = 502

Q. 2 hundred + 3 tens + 4 ones = 200 + 30 + 4 = 234

R. 9 hundreds + 1 ones = 900 + 3 + 903

S. 1 hundred + 5 tens + 3 ones = 100 + 50 + 3 = 153

So, the given set of numbers can be written in decreasing order as 903, 502, 234, 153,

i.e., R, P, Q, S

29. (C) : The place value of 5 is at tens place. The palace value of 7 is at hundreds place. The digit at ones place is the smallest one digit is 1

Hence, Meera's purse is having number 751

30. (B) : (A) 30 ones = 30: 3 tens = 30

So, 30 oness is equal to 3 tens.

(B) 20 ones = 200; 2 hundreds = 200

So, 200 ones is equal to 2 hundreds.

(C) 50 ones = 50; 5 tens = 50

So, 50 ones is equal to 5 tens

(D) 10 tens = 100; 100 ones = 100

So, 10 tens is equal to 100 one

Hence option (B) balance is incorrect.

1. (D) : Greatest number in the glass jar = 430

Smallest number in the glass jar = 155

So, sum = 430 - 155 = 585

2. (C) : $\boxed{3 + 3 + 3 + 3 + 3}$ = 15

So, ✳✳✳ + ✳✳✳ + ✳✳✳ + ✳✳✳ + ✳✳✳ is suitable

3. (D) : Greatest three digit

number is 999

Smallest three digit number is 100

Difference = 999 – 100 = 879

4. (D) : (A) 3 + 4 = 7; 5 + 2 = 7

Since 7 is equal to 7, so it is correct

(B) 20 – 7 = 13; 5 + 5 + 3 = 13

Since 13 is equal to 13, so it is correct

(C) 2 + 2 + 2 + 2 = 8; 20 – 12 = 8

Since 8 is equal to 8, so it is correct

(D) 50 – 7 = 43; 20 + 20 + 5 = 45

Since, 43 is not equal to 45, so it is incorrect

5. (A) : As 7 + 7 + 7 = 21

So, 3 groups of 7 is same as 21

6. (D) : (A) $\dfrac{70 + 40}{}$ = 70 + 4 = 110

(B) $\dfrac{80 + 25}{}$ = 80 + 25 = 105

(C) $\dfrac{95 + 10}{}$ = 95 + 10 = 105

(D) $\dfrac{85 + 12}{}$ = 85 + 12 = 97

So, Nandita will choose the note given in option (D)

7. (C) : Number of dots 1 lady bug has = 8

Number of dots 4 lady bug has = 8 + 8 + 8 + 8 = 32

8. (B) : (P) 20 ones + 40 tens + 30 ones = 450

(Q) 30 tens + 20 ones + 40 tens = 720

(R) 10 tens + 80 ones + 155 ones = 305

(S) 120 ones + 10 tens + 80 ones = 300

So, the correct descending order is; Q, P, R, S.

9. (B) : Numbers shown on the sheet are 835 and 743

∴ Difference = 835 – 743 = 92

10. (B) : There are 8 clips

Grouping of 8 clips in 2 groups so that each girl gets has equal number of clips can be done as

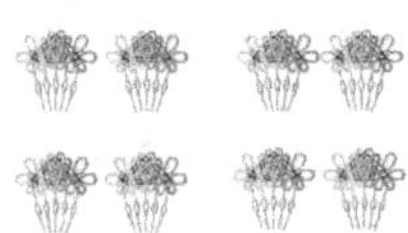

∴ Each girl gets 2 clips

11. (D) : We have $\triangle$ = 15

and $\square$ + $\triangle$ + $\triangle$ = 60

So, $\square$ + 15 + 15 = 60

Or 30 + 15 + 15 = 60

Hence $\square$ = 30

12. (B) : Subtracting 25 form 100 gives result 75.

13. (A) : Total number of marbles = 15

Number of crossed marbles = 3

So, the subtraction sentence will be 15 – 3 = 12

14. (B) : The numbers on the basket are 45, 7, 35 and 12

Sum of the numbers = 45 + 35 + 7 + 12 = 99

15. (D) : 24 + 3 = 27 and 18 + 3 = 21

From the options the number less than 27 but more than 21 is 25

16. (B) : Number of books 1 child has = 6

Number of books 50 children has = 300

Number of pencils 1 child has = 3

Number of pencils 50 children has = 150

Difference between the total number of books and pencils = 300 – 150 = 150

So, 150 more books are there than pencils

17. (A) : Sheela has 48 cakes

Grouping of 12 cakes into 4 groups so that each table has equal number of cakes can be done as

∴ Each table will have 12 cakes

18. (C) : 53 + 22 = 75

19. (D) : Number of cupcakes in 1 box = 8

Number of cupcakes in 8 boxes = 8 + 8 + 8 + 8 + 8 + 8 + 8 + 8 = 64

20. (C) : Number of ladoos in 1 tin = 6

Number of ladoos in 2 tins = 6 + 6 = 12

Number of ladoos Sonal has = 12

Number of ladoos Sonal gave to her sister = 8

So, number of laoods left with Sonal = 12 – 8 = 4

21. (B) : Number of mangoes Naman had = 37

Number of mangoes Vinay had = 63

Total number of mangoes = 37 + 63 = 100

22. (A) : Number of children in the playground = 243

Number of girls = 117

∴ Number of boys = 243 – 117 = 126

23. (C) : Number of flowers Muskan needs = 378

Number of flowers in the box = 228

Number of flowers to be bought = 378 – 228 = 150

24. (C) : Number of cherries

Meena has = 14

Meena gives 2 cherries to each of her 5 friends

So, She will give 2 + 2 + 2 + 2 + 2 = 10 cherries

Number of cherries, left with Meena = 14-10 =

25. (D) : Number of legs 1 duck has = 2

Number of legs 8 duck has = 2 + 2 + 2 + 2 + 2 + 2 + 2 + 2 = 16

26.
$$\begin{array}{r} 9\ 9 \\ -0\ 9 \\ \hline 9\ 0 \end{array}$$

So, R = 9 and S = 0

27. (C) : We have X + 75 = 100

or 25 + 75 = 100

So, X = 25

Now 100 – 18 = 82

So, Y = 82

Also Y + 28 = Z

$\Rightarrow$ 82 = 28 = Z

So, Z = 110

28. (D) : From the options 86 is an even number which is more than 70 and less than 90. It's ten's digit is greater than the one's digit

Also, the sum of its digit = 8 + 6 =14

29. (D) : Number of cookies sold on Thursday = 35

Number of cookies sold on Friday = 35 +35 = 70

Number of cookies sold on Monday = 70 + 70 + 70 +70 = 280

30. (B) : Given

☆ + ☆ + ☆ + ☆ + ☐ + ☐ = 88

And, ☆ + ☆ + ☐ + ☐ = 58

$\Rightarrow$ ☆ + ☆ + 58 = 88

$\Rightarrow$ ☆ + ☆ = 30 or 15 + 15 = 30

So, ☆ = 15

3 Length, Weight, Capacity and Temperature

1. (B) : Length of crayon P = 10 - 5 = 5 cm

Length of crayon Q = 8 - 2 = 6 cm

Length of crayon R = 9 - 5 = 4 cm

Length of crayon S = 6 - 2 = 4 cm

So, the length of the longest crayon is 6 cm

2. (B) : Cup Q is of 2 kg, which is the heaviest among all

3. (A) : We can fill 4 glasses of milk from 1 litre of milk

Then, 4 litres of milk can fill 4 + 4 + 4 + 4 = 16 glasses of milk

4. (D) : Temperature shown on the thermometer is 70° C

Fridge temperature is 15° C less than the temperature

shown on the thermometer

So, fridge temperature = 70° C - 15° C = 55° C

5. (C) : Weight of mangoes = (2 + 4) kg = 6 kg

    Weight of melons = (7 + 6 + 5) kg = 18 kg

6. (A) : Bowl can hold less capacity of juice

7. (A) : Hat S is the shortest

8. (C) : Weight of 1 ball = 100 g

    ∴ Weight of 5 balls = (100 + 100 + 100+ 100+ 100) = 500 g

9. (D) : Distance covered from class to market = 60m

    Distance covered from market to Home = 30m

    So, total distance covered = (60 + 30) = 90m

10. (A) : Weight of Watermelon = 2 kg

    Weight of Books = 5 kg

    (Therefore) Total weight of Watermelon and Books

    = (2 + 5) kg = 7 kg

11. (C) : Difference between the weight of Rice bag and books = (10 – 5) kg = 5 kg

12. (B) : Capacity of bucket = 6 litres

    Water filled in the bucket = 3 litres

    The bucket can contain 6 – 3 = 3 litres more water

13. (D) : Height of Monkey = 3 m

    Height of Giraffe = 10 m

    ∴ Difference = (10 – 3) = 7m

14. (D) : Bottle (a) contains 200ml of juice

    Bottle (b) contains 500ml of juice

    Bottle (c) contains 300ml of juice

    So, Bottles (b) contains more than 300ml of juice

15. (A) : Quantity of water the jug can hold = 5 + 2 + 1 = 8 litres

16. (A) : Quantity of juice in the jug = 6 liters

    Quantity of juice to be added = 10 - 6 = 4 litres

17. (B) : Quantity of milk Nitin drinks everyday = 1 litre

    Quantity of milk he drinks in 15 days

    = 1 + 1 + 1 + 1 + 1 + 1 + 1 + 1 + 1 + 1 + 1 + 1 + 1 + 1 + 1

    = 15 litre

18. (A) : We have

    🥭 + 🥭 + 🥭 = 450 g

    or, 150 + 150 + 150 = 450 g

    So, 🥭 = 150 g

19. (D) : Height of the crane = 35 m

    (A) 105 – 63 = 42

    (B) 62 – 34 = 28

    (C) 90 – 25 = 65

(D) 98 − 63 = 35

So, option D is same as the height of crane.

20. (C) : + 150 g = 50 g + 300 g + 150 g

$\Rightarrow$ + 150 g = 500 g

or, 350 g + 150 g = 500 g

$\Rightarrow$ = 500 g

So, the weight of melon = 350 g

21. (A) : Quantity of milk Rohan bought = 130 litres

Quantity of milk used = 90 litres

So, quantity of milk left = 130 − 90 = 40 litres

22. (A) : Number of bread loafs Manju baked = 9

Weight of each bread loaf = 4 kg

So, weight of 9 loaf altogether = 4 + 4 + 4 + 4 + 4 + 4 + 4 + 4 + 4 = 36 kg

23. (D) :

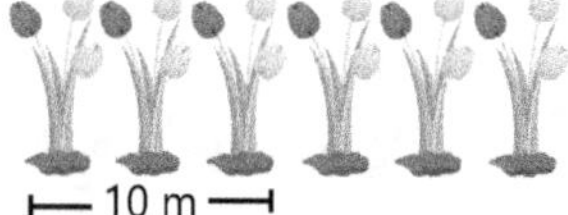

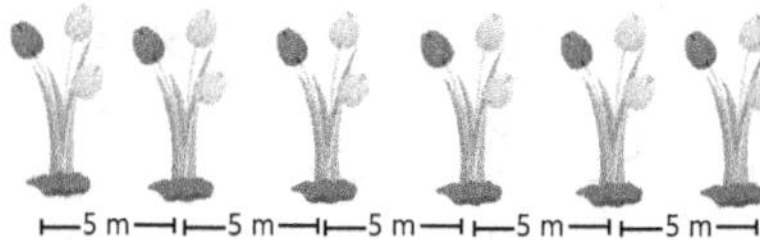

So, the distance between the third flower plants and the sixth flower plants = 5 + 5 + 5 = 15 m

24. (A) : Quantity of Milk in the tank = 82 litres

Quantity of Milk drained out = 35 litres

∴ Quantity of Milk left in the tank

= 82 − 35 = 47 litres

25. (B) : Number of jowar bags = 15

Weight of each jowar bag = 20 kg

Total weight of jowar bags

= 20 + 20 + 20 + 20 + 20 + 20 + 20 + 20 + 20 + 20 + 20 + 20 + 20 + 20 + 20 = 300 kg

26. (C) :

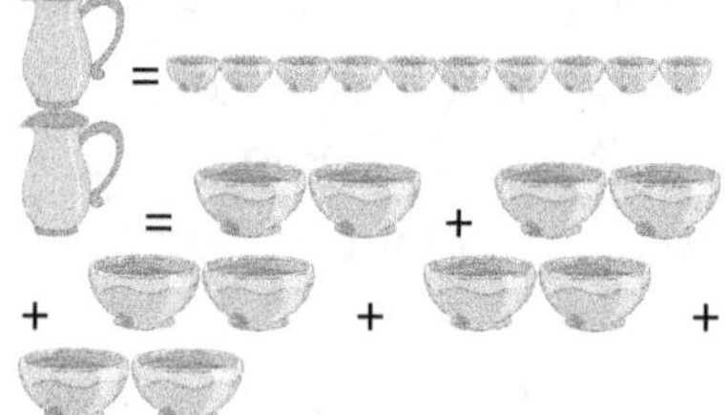

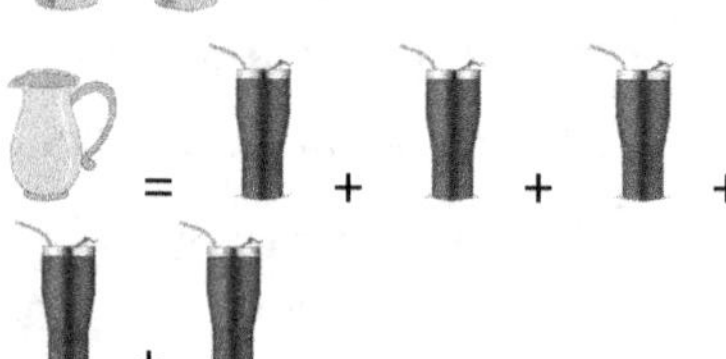

27. (B)

28. (B) : Distance travelled by 1st route = (450 + 295) = 745 m

Distance travelled by 2nd route = (350 + 422) = 802 m

∴ Difference = (802 − 745) = 57 m

So, 1st route was 57 m shorter than 2nd route

29. **(A)** : Quantity of milk in 1 small milk can = 1 litre

Quantity of milk in 1 large milk can = (8 + 1) = 9 litres

It is given that Aditya bought 4 small and 2 large milk cans

∴ Quantity of milk in 4 small milk cans

= (1 + 1 + 1 + 1) = 4 litres

Quantity of milk in 2 large milk cans = (9 + 9) = 18 litres

So, total quantity of milk Aditya bought

= (4 + 18) = 22 litres

30. **(A)** : Weight of rice bag = 46 kg

Weight of jowar bag is 10 kg less than rice bag

So, weight of jowar bag = (46 − 10) = 36 kg

Wheat bag weight is 2 kg less than rice bag

So, weight of wheat bag = (46 − 2) = 44 kg

Bajra bag weight is 7 kg more than jowar bag

So, weight of bajra bag = (36 − 7) = 43 kg

∴ rice bag weights the most.

4 Time and Money

1. **(B)** : Raghav starts his cricket practice on 1st October

If he practices only on odd number of days, then he practices for 15 days.

2. **(C)** : 10 minutes past 12:00 p.m. is 12:10 p.m.

3. **(A)** : The time is 10 minutes after 11 O'clock

4. **(B)** : The sum of five ₹ 10 notes and two ₹ 20 notes

= ₹ (10 + 10 + 10 + 10 +10 +20 + 20) = ₹ 90

5. **(A)** : ₹ 5 + ₹ 5 + ₹ 5 + ₹ 5 + ₹ 5 + ₹ 5 + ₹ 5 = ₹ 35

So, we need five ₹ 4 coins to make ₹ 35

6. **(A)** : Time showing in the clock = 8:30 p.m.

The clock is 10 minutes fast

∴ Actual time is 10 minutes before 8:30 p.m. which is 8:20 p.m.

7. **(A)** : Time at which Reena left her home = 8:30 p.m.

She waited 10 minutes for the bus.

So, the time at which Reena took the bus = 8:40 p.m.

Time at which Reena reached offfice = 9:40 p.m

So, duration of her journey was 1 hour 10 minutes

8. **(D)** : Time at which Samir started walking to the class = 3: 45 p.m

Time at which he reached the class = 4:05 p.m.

Time taken by him to walk to the class = 20 minutes

9. (B) : Geometry box is the costliest item, which costs ₹ 40

10. (D)

11. (C) : Total money required = ₹ (10 + 25 + 30 + 40) = ₹ 105

12. (D) : Cost of bag = ₹ 125

So, amount of money required to buy the bag is more than enough to buy the given bag

13. (B) : Time showing in the clock = 12:30 p. m.

The clock is 5 minutes slow

So, actual time should be 5 minutes after 12:30.pm. which is 12: 35 p.m.

14. (D) : The amount of money Ravi has = ₹ (50 + 50 + 10 + 5) = ₹ 115

15. (A) : 10 minutes after 12 noon is 12:10 p.m.

16. (C) : Starting time = 4:00 p.m.

Ending time – 5:30 p.m.

∴ Varun study for 1 hr 30 mins.

17. (A) : Cost of 1 pair of sandals = ₹ 180

Cost of 2 pairs of sandals = ₹ (180 + 180) = ₹ 360

18. (B) : Cost of 1 pair of sandals = ₹ 180

Cost of 2 shirts = ₹ (150 + 150) = ₹ 300

Difference = ₹ (300 – 180) = ₹ 120

So, one pair of sandals costs ₹ 120 less than two shirts

19. (A) : 1 hr 10 mins before 4 p.m. = 3:50 p.m

So, option D is same as the height of crane.

20. (C) : At 8:45 p.m., the hour hand of the clock will lie near to 9.

21. (C) : Time at which Anita reached the market = 10:40 a.m.

Time spend in the market = 1 hour 10 minutes

∴ Time at which she left the market is 1 hour 10 minutes after 10:40 a.m which 11:50 a.m.

22. (B) : Amount of money shown = ₹ (100 + 50 + 2 + 5) = ₹ 157

(A) 100 + 50 + 5 = 155

(B) One hundred fifty seven = 157

(C) 100 ones + 50 ones + 2 ones = 152

(D) One hundred + 5 ones = 105

So, option (B) is correct

23. (C) : Seema started driving at 7:30 p.m.

She reached her destination at 9:45 p.m.

Time taken to reach the

destination is 2 hours 15 minutes.

24. (D) : Amount of money Sheela has is `600

Cost of dress = ₹ 250, Cost of Tiara = ₹ 30

∴ Total cost = ₹ (250 + 30) = ₹ 280

Now, money left with Sheela = ₹ (600-280) = ₹ 320

25. (B) : Time taken by Anu to complete one round = 20 minutes

Time taken by Anu to complete three rounds = 20 + 20 + 20 = 60 minutes or 1 hour

26. (B) : Amount given = ₹ (100 + 50) = ₹ 150

Cost of wrist watch = ₹ 110

So, change received = ₹ (150 – 110) = ₹ 40

∴ P = ₹ 150, Q = ₹ 120, R = ₹ 40

Also, cost of belt = ₹ 120

So, P – 100 = S ∴ ₹ (150 – 120) = S

S = ₹ 30

27. (A)

28. (D) : Cost of cricket bat = ₹ 100

Cost of shoes = ₹ 220

Total cost of both the items = ₹ (150 + 220) = ₹ 370

29. (B) : From the given items

costliest item is Makeup kit and cheapest item is clips

Now, cost of makeup kit = ₹ 50

Cost of clips = ₹ 15

∴ Total cost = ₹ (50 + 15) = ₹ 65

Money given to the seller = ₹ 100

Money get back from the seller = ₹ (100 – 65) = ₹ 35

30. (D) : Rohan starts his cricket practice on 1st of July.

He practices for 15 days.

Every Sunday is a holiday.

So, his practice finishes on 17th July i.e. on Sunday.

5 Lines, Shapes and Solids

1. (C) : The triangle in the given figure are 6 in numbers

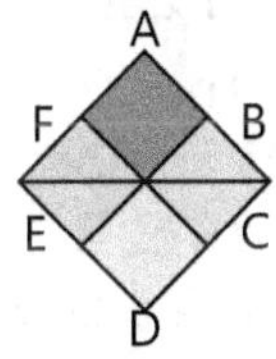

2. (A) : Curve line in the given figure are 4 in number

3. (D) : Square shape is missing

4. (B) : Number of triangles in the given figure are 10

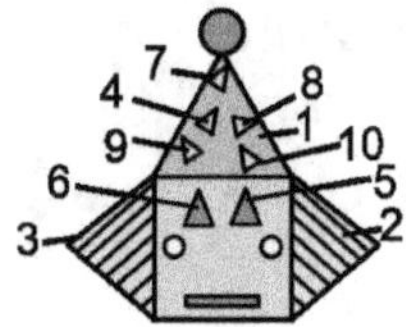

5. (A) : There are 11 straight lines in the given figure

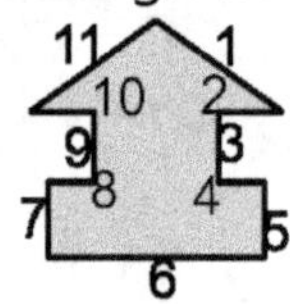

6. (A) : There are flat faces in the given figure

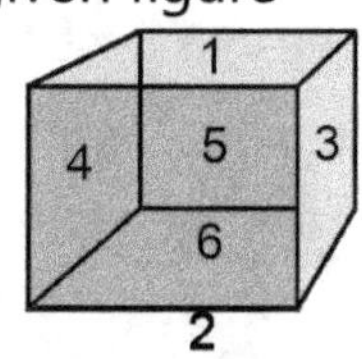

7. (C) : Shape S has the largest number of sides i.e. 6

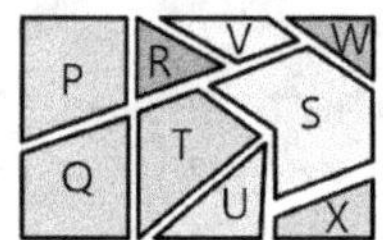

8. (A) : The straight lines required to form the given figure are AB, BC, CD, DA, BD, EF, FG, HI & IJ i.e. 9 in number

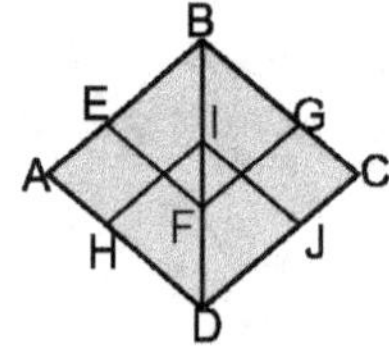

9. (B) : Rectangle

10. (A) : Given figure is formed by 4 curved lines

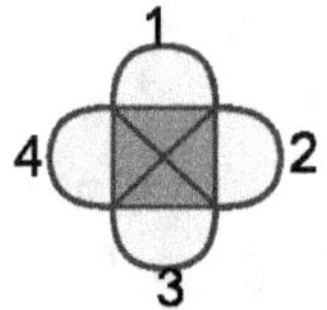

11. (A) : Number of curved lines = 4

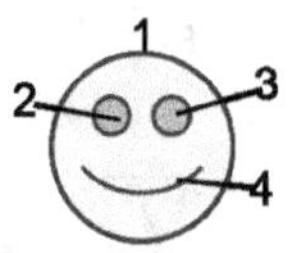

12. (C) : Number of squares = 11

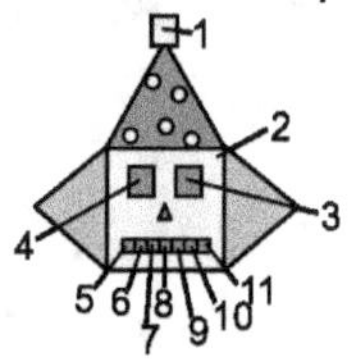

13. (C) : The below figure has squares, rectangles and circles but does not have any triangles

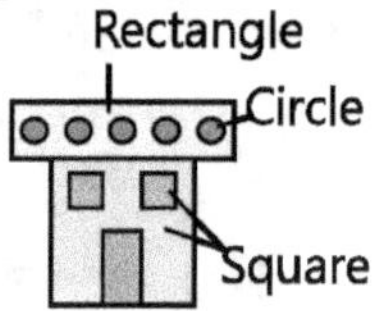

14. (B) : Number of slanting lines in the given figure = 8

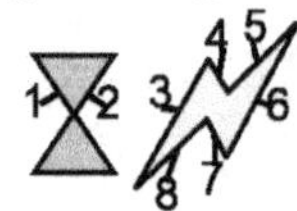

15. (A) : Number of in ⬭ the given figure = 7

16. (B) : Number of squares in the given figure = 5

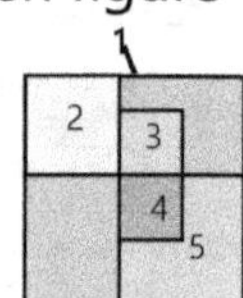

17. (C) : Number of sleeping lines in the given figure = 8

18. (B) : 12 straight line are required to make the given figure

19. (B) : 3 curved lines and 2 straight line

20. (A) : The given figure has 6 curved lines

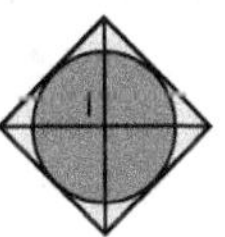 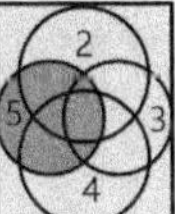 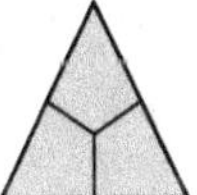

21. (B) : Circles in the stickers are 5 in numbers

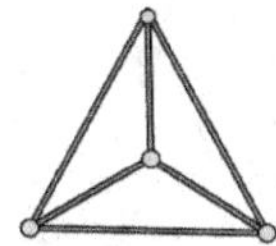

22. (B) :

23. (D) : The figure formed is as follows:

24. (C) : The squares in the flag are 9 in numbers

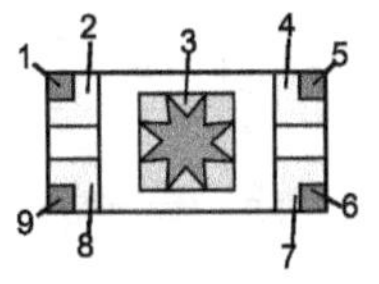

25. (B) :

26. (D) : Figure in option A has 12 unit squares

Figure in option B has 8 unit squares

Figure in option C has 14 unit squares

Figure in option D has 6 unit squares

So, option D has minimum number of squares

27. (D)

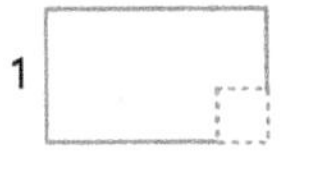  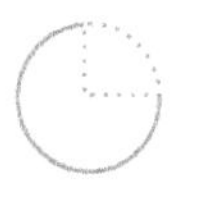

28. (D) : 6 , 4

29. (B) : Manisha chooses those shapes which are made up of only curved lines

30. (D) : The figure is made up of 4 triangles, 4 squares and 1 rectangle.

6 Patterns

1. (A) : 15, 19, 13, 27, 31

   +4 +4 +4 +4 +4

2. (B) : 22, 33, 44, 55, 66, 77

   +11 +11 +11 +11 +11

3. (C) : 14, 28, 42, 56, 70, 84

   +14 +14 +14 +14 +14

4. (A) : 14, 20, 35, 55, 80, 110
   +10 +15 +20 +25 +30

5. (C) : 50, 100, 250, 350, 450, 550
   +100 +100 +100 +100 +100

6. (B) : 6, 11, 16, 21, 26
   +5 +5 +5 +5

7. (C) : 110, 115, 125, 130, 140, 145, 155
   +5 +10 +5 +10 +5 +10

8. (C) : 500, 520, 540, 560, 580, 600
   +20 +20 +20 +20 +20

9. (C) : 527, 530, 533, 536, 539
   +3 +3 +3 +3

10. (A) : 220, 215, 205, 200, 190, 185
   -5 -10 -5 -10 -5

11. (C) : 215, 200, 185, 170, 155
   -15 -15 -15 -15

12. (B) : 125, 225, 325, 425, 524, 625
   +100 +100 +100 +100 +100

13. (D) : 8, 16, 24, 32, 40, 48
   +8 +8 +8 +8 +8

14. (A) : 115, 125, 135, 145, 155, 165, 175, 185, 195
   +10 +10 +10 +10 +10 +10 +10 +10

15. (D) : 80, 70, 61, 53, 46, 40, 35
   -10 -9 -8 -7 -6 -5

16. (C) : The pattern ★ ▬ ▲ is repeated

17. (A) : Each figure repeat itself after three figures

18. (B) : The pattern repeat itself after every fourth figure.
   So, the missing figure is ◆

19. (A) : The pattern repeat itself after every fourth figure

20. (A) : The pattern repeat itself after every 2nd figure

21. (C)

22. (A) : The pattern ☺ ☹ 😐 is repeated

23. (A) : Number of stars are increasing by one in each step

24. (A) : The pattern is repeated
   Also, smaller stars inside the figures becomes unshaded and shaded in each alternate step

25. (D) : The pattern repeat itself after every fourth figure.

26. (C)

27. (B)

28. (A) : The pattern repeat itself after every fourth figure.

29. (D) : The pattern repeat itself after every fourth figure.

30. (D) : Each figure repeat itself after every third figure.

1. (B) : ⬠ = 4
   So, ⬠ ⬠ ⬠ ⬠

2. (C) :  $= 14$

So,

$= 14 + 14 + 14 = 42$

3. (C) : 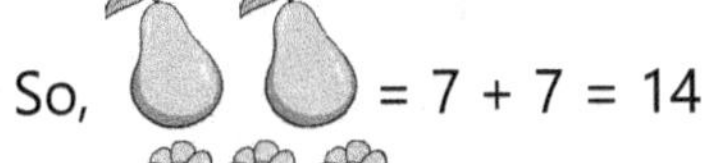 $= 28$

or $7 + 7 + 7 + 7 = 28$

So,  $= 7 + 7 = 14$

4. (B) : = 26

$26 + 26 = 52$

5. (D) : Maximum number of students are in class 4 – D, i.e., 50 students

6. (C) : Section 4 – B and 4 – C have the same number of students i.e., 30 students.

7. (A) : Number of student in class 4 – A = 40

Number of student in class 4 – B = 30

Number of student in class 4 – C = 30

Number of student in class 4 – D = 50

Total number of students in class 4 = 40 + 30 + 30 + 50 = 150

8. (A) : Number of bracelets beaded by Anita = 27

Number of bracelets beaded by Anju = 33

∴ Number of bracelets beaded by Anita and Anju = 27 + 33 = 60

9. (C) : Number of bracelets beaded by Preeti = 30

Number of bracelets beaded by Riya = 15

Number of fewer bracelets beaded by Riya than Preeti = 30 – 15 = 30

10. (C) : Most boys prefer colouring book

11. (A) : Number of boys prefer colouring book = 90

Number of boys prefer comic book = 60

Number of boys prefer colouring book more than comic book = 90 – 60 = 30

12. (A) : Jay got minimum trophies. i.e., 2 trophies

13. (B) : Anil and Monika got same number of trophies.

i.e. 4 trophies each.

14. (C) : Number of trophies Minal got = 10

Number of trophies Ansh got = 6

∴ Number of trophies Minal got more than

Ansh = 10 – 6 = 4

15. (A) Number of television Mr. Warma sold in March = 45

16. (A) : The least number of televisions were sold in April.

i.e., 30 televisions

17. (C) : Number of televisions sold in May = 75

Number of televisions April = 30

∴ Number of televisions sold in May

more than in April = 75 – 30 = 45

18. (B) : Number of girls who prefer pink colour = 32

Number of girls who prefer yellow colour = 26

Number of girls who prefer pink colour more

than yellow colour = 32 – 26 = 6

19. (A) : Yellow colour is least likes by girls

20. (A) : Number of girls who prefer orange colour = 24

Number of girls who prefer Maroon colour = 16

∴ Number of girls who prefer orange and

Maroon colour altogether = 24 + 16 = 40

21. (D) Number of toys sold in May = 18

Number of toys sold in June = 8

Number of toys sold in July = 20

Number of toys sold in August = 22

∴ Total number of toys sold in four month altogether

= 18 + 8 +20 +22 = 68

22. (D) : Number of toys sold in May = 18

Number of toys sold in June = 8

∴ Number of toys sold in May more

than in June = 18 -8 = 10

23. (C) : Number of children who prefer

playing badminton = 4 + 4 + 4 + 4 + 4 = 20

24. (A) : Cricket is most popular

25. (D) : Number of children who prefer cycling

= 4 + 4 + 4 + 4 + 4 + 4 + 4 = 28

Number of children who prefer swimming

= 4 + 4 + 4 + 4 = 16

∴ Number of children who prefer cycling

more than swimming = 28 – 16 = 12

26. (B) : Number of burgers sold on Thursday = 30

Varun sold each burger for ₹ 2.

So, money collected on Thursday = ₹ 60

Number of burgers sold on

Wednesday = 20

Money collected on Wednesday = ₹ 40

So, money collected on Thursday more than

on Wednesday = ₹ (60 – 40) = ₹ 20

27. (B)

28. (A) : Total number of participants for

    Marathon and 400 m relay = 10 + 20 = 30

    Also, the number of participants for high jump = 30

29. (D) : From the given data, it is clear that

    Rohan planted maximum number trees, i.e., 28 trees

    Option A is incorrect

    Samira planted more number of trees than

    Varun is incorrect, as both planted the same number

    of trees, i.e., 20 trees and Aarti planted the most

    number of trees. i.e., 16 trees. It is also incorrect

    Reena planted 20 trees is correct

    So option D is correct

30. (D) : Number of cards Sneha collected = 300

    Number of cards Sanjeevani collected = 250

Number of cards Lata collected = 400

Number of cards Usha collected = 200

1. (C) : The given pattern contains 3 identical groups.

    Each group has 3 identical images and 1 different image.

    So, the pattern can be shown with 3 same letters and 1 different letter.

2. (B) : The shapes having number of sides equal to 4 are P, Q, T, V and X

3. (C) : Rajan starts his practice on 1st August.

    It ends after 15 days (and all Sundays are holidays) i.e. on 18th August

    So, his practice finishes on Monday

4. (D) : Kite in option D is exactly same as that of the given kite

5. (A) : Counting toy P has the least number of rings.

6. (B) : Block P is heavier than block Q.

    Block S is heavier than block P

    Block Q is heavier than Block R

    So, the arrangement from heaviest to lightest is S, P, Q,

R

7. (D) : Since 6 appears minimum number of times on the wheel. So, it is less likely to come.

8. (D) : If day before yesterday was Thursday

then yesterday was Friday and today is Saturday.

So, tomorrow will be Sunday.

9. (D) : The pattern repeat itself after every third figure.

So, the next figure is (Image of the star with heart shape)

10. (C) : Alphabet M is in the middle of the given word

11. (D) : According to the given information

we have Soham > Arun > Manthan > Rohit

So. Soham is the tallest

12. (A) : Figure in option A is made up of only curved lines, while other figures are made up of standing lines, sleeping lines, and slanting lines

13. (C) : Number of triangles in the figure = 24

Number of circles in the figure = 6

So, there are 24 − 6 = 18 triangles than circles

14. (A) : Weight of toy duck is equal to the weight of toy car.

15. (B) The pattern is;

14 19 24 29 34 39 44

+5 +5 +5 +5 +5 +5

16. (C) : Alphabet T is embedded in the given figure

17. (B) : Square s formed by standing lines and sleeping lines, but here standing lines are called sleeping lines and sleeping lines are called curved lines. So, the square is formed by sleeping lines and curved lines.

18. (D) : 3rd Number from the left end is Number C.

And fourth to the right of Number C is Number G

19. (C) : 7 curved lines

20. (B) : In all figures except in option (B), the shapes inside the figure are made up of curved lines

21. (C)

22. (C) : The number of lines in the figure are equal to the number of sides of the figure

23. (C) :

24. (D) : We have, (Image of grapes)

So, there are 4 equal groups of 12 grapes

25. (A) :

26. (D) : After removing the cycle the new arrangement is

So, doll is at the fifth position from the left end

27. (B) The king of fruits is but here means

28. (C) : Circle

29. (C) : So, 4 equal groups of 5 candles each can be formed from the given candles

30. (A) : The rule followed is;

3 + 5 + 7 + 9 = 24

2 + 10 + 5 + 3 = 20

So, 8+ 5 + 3 +2 = 18